TIME MANAGEMENT AND LIFE SKILLS FOR TEENS

MASTER STUDY HABITS & SET EPIC GOALS

JAY MEELA

DISCLAIMER

This book is designed to guide and give teenagers practical insights into enhancing various aspects of their lives. Its purpose is to empower young readers with knowledge and strategies to improve their daily routines, relationships, and overall well-being. The content of this book is focused solely on offering advice, tips, and techniques related to personal development and life improvement for teenagers. It does not pertain to spiritual or philosophical matters.

Real-life anecdotes, examples, and scenarios may be included in this book to illustrate key concepts and inspire reflection. These stories are intended solely for the purpose of enhancing comprehension and practical application of the life hacks discussed in the text. No association with specific individuals or events should be implied unless explicitly stated in the text.

The author and publisher are not responsible for any misinterpretation or misuse of the advice and strategies presented in this book. Readers are urged to exercise discretion, consider their unique situations, and consult with relevant professionals when necessary before implementing any suggestions.

I encourage teenagers to approach this book with an open mind and a willingness to explore new ideas and habits that can contribute to personal growth and success.

To my dearest Daughter Kylee,

As you journey through the vibrant years of your teens, This book is a token of my love and belief in your incredible potential. Within these pages, you'll find guidance and wisdom to navigate the exciting challenges ahead. Remember, every moment is a new opportunity to grow, learn and pursue your dreams. Cherish your time, make the most of your abilities, and let your aspirations soar high.

With all my love and support,
J-Dad

CONTENTS

"You can't have a better tomorrow if you are thinking about yesterday all the time"

— CHARLES KETTERING

INTRODUCTION

Growing up, even the simplest chores felt like a burden to me. From making the bed to putting my dishes back into the sink, and even something as trivial as closing the door behind me! Yes, one could say I wasn't the role model kid, but in hindsight, I am often surprised at how patient my father used to be with me.

He used to ask me sternly yet very politely if I made the bed, did my homework, put my stuff back where I picked it up from, and more. Most often, this politeness was what got to me, and I would do everything by the book, but sometimes I would simply forget.

And sometimes, when I woke up on the wrong side of the bed (*pun intended*), I would remember but still wouldn't make my bed. "Why bother?" I would ask myself. "I'm going to mess it up again soon. It's not like I have guests coming over."

Of course, when my father would see this, he would ask me to do it regardless. He would say, "Making your bed is like a trigger-start for your routine. It will set the tone for your entire day. Think of it as the first step toward 'making your day,' not just your bed."

At the time, I would dismiss it, as I'm sure everyone will. Begrudgingly, I would do it, but never really from the heart. But getting older, having responsibilities, and a daughter of my own to teach, I understand how his statements were backed by wisdom, not just a way to make me do my chores.

Making my bed in the morning, putting stuff back where I got it from, and putting dishes in the sink were sort of milestones—small accomplishments that marked the completion of a task. Simply looking around the room after making the bed would always give me a sense of accomplishment (which I dismissed at the time). The neat, tidy room marked the beginning of the day and set the tone of the day by giving me a win early in the morning.

But why are we talking about making your bed? After all, this book isn't just about housekeeping skills. It's about something much bigger - mastering time management and life skills. So, what's the connection?

These little daily routines, like making your bed, are like the building blocks of a well-organized life. They may seem trivial, but they set the stage for more significant achievements. I've discovered that the same principles that my father instilled in me, which began with simple chores, can be applied to your entire life. And you know what? Studies back this up, too.

Right now, you might be facing some challenges. You're juggling school, extracurricular activities, maybe even a part-time job, and it feels like you're always running out of time. You want to do well in your classes, enjoy your hobbies, and have fun, but it's a constant struggle.

Or maybe you've joined a club or sports team that you're incredibly passionate about, but your grades are slipping, and you're too scared to ask for help. You're worried your parents might pull you out of your activities to focus solely on academics.

And perhaps, college is on the horizon, and you're eager to get into a good one. You want your college applications to stand out with impressive achievements and soft skills that set you apart from the crowd.

But maybe you've convinced yourself you're just "naturally disorganized." You've tried various time management techniques, but none seem to work. You think you work best under pressure, even though it often feels like a never-ending struggle.

That's why you're here. This book isn't just about making your bed but taking control of your life. It's about setting a positive tone for each day and achieving the success you've always dreamed of.

THE RIPPLE EFFECT OF SMALL HABITS

Think of your daily routines as the building blocks of your life. Like building a tower from LEGO bricks, each small piece contributes to the overall structure. While a single LEGO brick might not seem impressive on its own, together, they create something substantial.

Likewise, positive habits, even the most basic ones like making your bed or organizing your desk, have a ripple effect. They set the tone for your day, creating a sense of accomplishment, order, and control. This sense of achievement in the morning can affect your mindset and productivity throughout the day.

DISCIPLINE & RESPONSIBILITY

One of the essential life skills that these habits nurture is discipline. Discipline isn't about being strict or overly regimented; it's about developing the self-control and determination to stick to your goals. It's about choosing the long-term benefits over short-term comfort. Making your bed every morning requires discipline. It's a commitment to doing something small consistently.

When you make your bed, you take responsibility for your personal space. You're acknowledging that this space is your domain, and you're in charge of keeping it tidy and organized. This is a simple act, but it instills a sense of responsibility that can extend to other areas of your life, such as your schoolwork, relationships, and future goals.

TIME MANAGEMENT AND PRIORITIZATION

Another life skill that these habits build is effective time management. Let's say you decide to organize your backpack before going to bed. You're not just arranging books and pens but preparing for the next day's challenges. This act of preparation teaches you to plan ahead, prioritize tasks, and allocate your resources efficiently.

Moreover, small positive habits help you optimize your routines. When you make your bed, for instance, it sets a structure for your morning. You start your day with a simple accomplishment and a clear space, which can boost your productivity. This is an invaluable skill that can be applied to managing your time effectively, ensuring you have time for studies, extracurricular activities, and leisure without feeling overwhelmed.

RESILIENCE & ADAPTABILITY

Life is full of surprises and challenges. Building and maintaining positive habits instills resilience and adaptability. You're better equipped to handle disruptions and unexpected setbacks when you've established a routine of good habits.

For instance, let's say you always clean your workspace before starting your homework. But one day, you can't find your favorite pen or your computer crashes, and you have to change your plan. Having a habit of organization and a clear routine makes you better prepared to adapt to such situations without losing your cool.

THE LONG-TERM BENEFITS

But the real magic happens in the long term. The little positive habits you develop now are not just building blocks for your teenage years but the foundation for your future success. As you grow, you'll find that these small daily routines have turned into indispensable life skills.

The discipline, responsibility, time management, and adaptability you acquire through these habits will be your allies in high school, college, and the workforce. They will help you excel academically, thrive in your career, and maintain healthy relationships.

In the chapters that follow, we'll explore specific techniques and strategies to nurture and expand these habits. We'll take a closer look at time management, goal setting, and soft skills that are key to your personal and professional growth.

Remember, *success doesn't happen overnight*. It's a result of consistent effort and often starts with the small, daily habits you cultivate. So, let's continue this journey of transforming these positive habits into life skills that will empower you now and carry you toward a future full of achievement and fulfillment.

When you read this book, you'll discover a variety of time management and productivity techniques. We're not about a one-size-fits-all approach. You'll find strategies like the Pomodoro Technique, the Maker vs. Manager Schedules, the Rule of 52 and 17 for breaks, and much more. The idea is to explore these options and find the strategy that works best for you.

But you might be wondering, "*Why should I listen to Jay Meela?*" Well, I'm not just an author; I'm also a stepdad to a teenage girl. I've been where you are. I've seen the struggles, the doubts, and the late-night study sessions. I understand the challenges teenagers face today.

Before I came across the strategies I'm about to share with you, I had my fair share of difficulties. It was tough to balance work, family, and personal goals. But with time, patience, and the right knowledge, I found a way to make it work. And I'm here to help you do the same.

This is the right book for you because it's not just about time management; it's about your journey toward becoming the best version of yourself. So, grab a cup of your favorite beverage, get comfortable, and let's master time management and life skills, setting epic goals, and achieving your dreams.

Are you ready? I'm here to guide you every step of the way. Let's get started on this exciting journey together.

1

TIME SCARCITY – THE MYSTERY OF THE ELUSIVE HOURS

"Time is a created thing. To say 'I don't have time' is like saying 'I don't want to."

— LAO TZU

Have you ever wondered why, despite having more leisure time and shorter work hours compared to our counterparts from 50 years ago, it often feels like there's never enough time? In a world filled with gadgets designed to save time and make life more efficient, we find ourselves perpetually caught in the grips of the elusive ticking clock.

As a child, it felt like every minute and every second of my life was spent *doing* something. Even when I was playing Dangerous Dave, it felt like I had something to do. In hindsight, that was me wasting hours, but it felt really important at the time. Sort of like a rough routine, if you could call that.

Sunday afternoons at my grandparent's house were no different, either. After lunch, my grandfather would take out his chessboard. He would set up the pieces with the utmost care, polishing each one ever-so-gently before placing it right in the middle of a square. We would then head on a slow, thoughtful game of chess.

Those games felt like they lasted for an eternity. We would move the pieces, engage in deep conversations about life, and enjoy the simple pleasure of each other's company. It was a stark contrast to the rest of my bustling week, where every minute seemed filled with tasks and activities.

Judy Wajcman, a professor of sociology at the London School of Economics, has coined this phenomenon as the "Time-Pressure Paradox." It's a curious paradox where we perceive a lack of time despite having more leisure hours at our disposal than ever before. To dive deeper into the concept of "not enough time," let's examine the primary reasons behind it.

TIME IS FIXED

As Nate Klemp – a philosopher, writer, and mindfulness entrepreneur – aptly puts it, "*you can't combat the acceleration of time by getting a faster phone, a better computer, or the perfect app. This isn't an external game. Time doesn't work like dollars in a bank account. Everyone gets the same 24 hours in a day.*"

Time is a finite resource, like a pizza. If you and your friends share a pizza, you each get a finite number of slices. You can savor them, but you can't magically create more. Focusing on tasks becomes a challenge in our distracted era with shrinking attention spans. Our brains now prefer quick, digestible activities, impacting extended focus.

In fact, in today's day and age, the attention span of an average human has decreased quite a lot (by almost 25% from 2000 to 2015). In 2000, it was 12.5 seconds. In 2015, it was found to be 8.25 seconds. And in 2023, it is expected to be even less. Compare that to a goldfish's attention span, standing at 9 seconds. What does the low attention span mean, though? It means we live in a world bombarded with distractions, from social media notifications to the constant allure of new messages and updates.

Unlike work, time is finite. Attempting to save time is like catching a falling leaf with chopsticks—possible but unsustainable. Yet, it's simpler than it seems; effective time management is achievable for anyone determined enough.

TIME IS LINEAR

In a world where technology enables us to edit and manipulate various aspects of our lives, the concept of linear time remains challenging to fully grasp. Time flows irreversibly; once a moment passes, it cannot be undone or revisited.

This inherent aspect of time creates a sense of scarcity, unlike the 'Undo' option in document editing. The challenge is akin to trying to change the temperature in an oven incrementally, where impatience can make moments feel excessively prolonged.

Our perception of time as an adversary that should move faster contributes to this sense of scarcity. Unfortunately, time maintains its constant pace, whether we're exercising, watching the clock during a plank, or engrossed in video gaming. To enhance productivity and alleviate the impact of time scarcity, a harmonious relationship with time is essential.

This brings us to the *"Arrow of Time."* In the world of physics, most interactions follow what is known as time-reversal invariance. This means that the laws of physics are symmetric whether you run the clock forward or backward.

To illustrate this, imagine watching the Earth rotate on its axis or orbiting the Sun. Observing these celestial motions makes it impossible to discern whether time is moving forward or in reverse. The same fundamental principles apply, and it's a key characteristic of time-reversal invariance.

You can think of it as the laws of physics being indifferent to the direction of time, just like an arrow would be indifferent to the falling leaves. However, when we step into the macroscopic world, something peculiar happens.

Events like a glass shattering or an egg cooking seem to have an inherent direction: forward. The time-reversed versions of these events, where glass pieces spontaneously assemble or an uncooked egg uncooks, never occur. It's as if the Universe holds a preferred direction, and this arrow of time aligns with the thermodynamic arrow. When looking at these everyday occurrences, it's clear that the Universe isn't time-reversal invariant, which gives rise to what's known as the thermodynamic arrow of time.

TIME MANAGEMENT IS A SKILL

A persistent feeling of time scarcity often stems from the fact that time management is a skill that requires cultivation rather than an innate trait. According to a 2022 study by Acuity Training in the UK, less than 20% of individuals follow a proper time management system, and only one in five conducts a monthly time audit. Even adults grapple with mastering this skill, highlighting the challenges faced by teenagers who may feel overwhelmed and disorganized.

Transitioning from the paradox of time scarcity, the journey into effective time management unfolds. In the upcoming sections, we will examine tools and strategies to conquer the time-pressure paradox. We will open up the secrets to maximizing the finite 24 hours each day for a future marked by achievement, not anxiety.

Beyond the ticking clock's hands, psychological and societal factors contribute to our constant sense of time scarcity. While it's common to attribute this pressure to a lack of hours a day, research challenges this notion. A 2011 survey indicated that roughly half of Americans rarely had free time. Yet, more recent studies suggest a slight improvement, revealing a paradox of feeling time-poor despite increased leisure time.

Contrary to the belief that fast-paced lifestyles contribute to time pressure, research spanning decades indicates otherwise. Americans worked three hours less per week from 1965 to 2003, and leisure time has increased. Recent Australian research dispels the illusion of time pressure, highlighting a significant gap between essential tasks and actual schedules, particularly notable among households without children.

This revelation emphasizes the role of personal choices in time allocation. While it's impractical to sacrifice well-being or minimal attention to family, it highlights the potential to reassess how we allocate time for work, chores, and other activities. Time pressure is influenced by these choices and our beliefs about how time should be spent, revealing a deeper connection between our psychology and societal expectations about time.

Enjoyment & Passion:

Research has highlighted the significant role that the enjoyment and passion we experience in our daily activities play in our perception of time pressure.

A 2004 Ohio study highlighted gender disparities in housework and volunteering, indicating that men experienced less time pressure and depression compared to women. The research suggested that men often engage in more enjoyable activities, creating a sense of accomplishment. Days filled with enjoyable tasks feel less stressful, highlighting the need to incorporate engaging activities into schedules to alleviate time pressure.

So, if you're continually feeling time-poor, it might result from not enjoying the activities or not being physical enough in your schedule. By adding more engaging and enjoyable tasks to your day, you might alleviate this feeling of time pressure.

Inner Conflict:

Conflicting goals create stress and time pressure, a phenomenon explored in a study revealing that thoughts of conflicting goals, such as saving money versus luxury purchases, elevate stress and anxiety.

Societal norms influence to-do lists, contributing to internal struggles, particularly evident in the expectations placed on mothers. Assessing tasks inducing inner conflict helps determine their worth and minimizes stress.

As a result, you find yourself with a limited number of hours in a day to accommodate all these expectations. Suppose a particular task induces a significant sense of inner conflict. In that case, it might be worthwhile to consider whether it's worth the stress.

A Sense of Control:

Perceived time pressure often accompanies a lack of control over one's schedule, as identified in a 2007 study highlighting reactive and active time management styles. Reactive individuals feel less in control, experiencing heightened time pressure, while active managers structure their days, reducing time-related stress.

Perceiving a lack of control over your time contributes to the feeling of being in a time bind. If you're in this situation, you might benefit from taking steps to regain control over your time, such as optimizing your to-do list or learning to say "no" to requests that don't align with your priorities.

The Value of Your Time:

The value attributed to time influences time perception, with high-income individuals more likely to feel time-poor. Even without additional work hours, a feeling of affluence intensifies time pressure.

Scarce resources, such as time, increase perceived value, as demonstrated in an experiment where students charging $1.50 per minute felt more time-pressured. Understanding these psychological nuances empowers effective time management, emphasizing the need for a fulfilling relationship with time beyond task completion.

These insights collectively reveal that the time pressure we experience is a complex interplay of psychology and societal norms. Understanding these factors can empower us to tackle time management more effectively.

We can establish a healthier relationship with our time by addressing the subjective elements contributing to time pressure. Time management is not solely about fitting more tasks into our day; it's about finding fulfillment and satisfaction in spending our precious hours. In the sections that follow, we'll explore practical strategies and insights to help you conquer time pressure, make the most of your finite 24 hours each day, and regain control over your time.

THE TIME BALANCING ACT – BEING BUSY BUT PRIORITIZING

Have you ever heard the one about the teen trying to balance school, social life, and hobbies all at once? Well, they didn't walk into a bar. But they sure stumbled into the world of time management, where finding balance often feels as tricky (if not more) as trying to juggle bowling balls and feathers.

Being a teenager isn't all fun and games, though we wish it were. The days can feel like a never-ending circus, with schoolwork, extracurricular activities, social gatherings, and self-care routines all vying for the spotlight. It's like trying to keep plates spinning while riding a unicycle.

It's not always obvious what's truly important and why there seem to be too many things to consider. That's where the planning fallacy comes into play. It often leads to time-related slip-ups but is something that can be managed with the dynamic nature of life. Motivation (or the lack thereof) and differences in learning and thinking can play into the time management puzzle as a teen.

Juggling Too Many Things That Are "Important" or "Urgent"

In the chaotic whirlwind of being a teenager, a perplexing issue often creeps up like an unexpected pop quiz—trying to decipher what's genuinely important. It's like attempting to solve a riddle with constantly changing rules.

Imagine you're faced with two tasks:

1. Completing a critical school report and
2. Attending Johnny's soccer practice. Which takes precedence?

That's where the conundrum begins.

The first challenge we confront is that what's important may not always be obvious. In this time management game, your preferences may not be as clear-cut as you'd like. You need to consider a decision theory. It involves determining the "utility function." Or, in simpler terms, think about what you genuinely want. When it's unclear what you're looking for, making the right choices becomes a puzzle.

But the complexities don't stop there. There's also an additional challenge: "Too many things to consider." With a seemingly endless array of tasks vying for your time, from schoolwork and social gatherings to errands and hobbies, it can feel like trying to corral a room full of energetic puppies.

Even if you had a comprehensive list of all these commitments and your own constraints and preferences, you'd face what computer scientists describe as an "intractable computational problem." In simpler words, there's no quick, one-size-fits-all algorithm for deciding how best to allocate your precious time.

So, what do you do?

You need to strike a balance between what's important and what's urgent. This is a critical skill for mastering the art of time management. Here's some guidance to help you strike a balance. If you'd like, you can turn these into steps or a checklist to help you on-the-go.

1. Define Your Priorities:

  a. Identify long-term goals and steps to achieve them.
  b. Use the "Eat That Frog" concept to tackle challenging tasks first.

2. Eisenhower's Matrix:

a. Categorize tasks into Urgent and Important, Important but Not Urgent, Urgent but Not Important, and Neither Urgent nor Important.
b. Use the infographic for quick reference.

"Urgent & Important" (Do First)

This is the VIP area! This is where your most urgent and important tasks hang out. Think of it as a party you can't miss. It's where you tackle fires, meet deadlines, and save the day. To conquer this quadrant, focus on time-sensitive and high-impact tasks. Your motto here: "Do it now!"

"Not Urgent but Important" (Schedule)

Your secret garden of productivity. It's filled with tasks that don't scream for your attention but are incredibly important for long-term success. Think of it as planting seeds that will grow into mighty oaks. These tasks include personal growth, skill-building, and quality time with loved ones. Plan, prioritize, and schedule these activities.

"Urgent but Not Important" (Delegate)

Now, you're in the land of distractions. These tasks are like shiny objects that beg for your focus but, truth be told, they're not all that important. Delegate when you can, because your time is precious. If you can't delegate, keep these tasks efficient and brief. Think of it as your own episode of "Mission: Distraction Possible."

"Not Urgent and Not Important" (Don't)

This is the "Don't Bother" zone. This is where time-wasters and energy-drainers lurk. These tasks neither scream for your attention nor contribute to your goals. It's your chill-out area, but beware of overindulging. The secret here: Don't spend too much time here. Stay focused on your top priorities and leave this quadrant for well-deserved breaks and relaxation.

3. Create a To-Do List:

    a. Break your day into manageable chunks.

    b. Prioritize tasks based on importance.

4. Time Blocking:

    a. Dedicate specific blocks of time to important tasks.

    b. Consider the Pomodoro Technique for focused work intervals.

5. Learn to Say No:

    a. Resist overcommitting to safeguard time for top priorities.

6. Delegate:

    a. Efficiently use available resources by delegating tasks.

7. Seek Guidance:

    a. Consult parents, mentors, or trusted advisors for valuable insights.

So, embrace the challenge, learn from it, and you'll soon find yourself mastering the delicate art of balancing "important" and "urgent" tasks in your daily life.

The Planning Fallacy – Taming Time's Trickster

After conquering the problem of identifying what's truly important, there's another tricky time management obstacle to jump over: the Planning Fallacy. Think of this as the mischievous time trickster that resides in you and loves to lead you astray.

Imagine this scenario: you've got a school project due in a week, and you seem to have ample time. Your brain confidently whispers, "I've got this." So, you delay starting the project. But, as the deadline looms closer, panic sets in, and you end up pulling an all-nighter. This has happened to me more times than I care to admit!

The culprit? *The Planning Fallacy.*

Here's the deal: we're all overly optimistic when estimating how much time tasks will take. Our brains tend to downplay the effort and challenges involved, leading us to believe we can finish things faster than we can. This is why you think you can write that 10-page paper in two hours (trust us, it's not happening).

But wait, there's more. The Planning Fallacy has a partner in crime, something known as "*the ostrich effect.*" It's when we deliberately ignore past experiences and pretend that deadlines don't exist. We bury our heads in the sand, believing we'll magically pull off a last-minute victory.

And that often costs us a lot in the short and medium term – also the long term in some instances.

A Study In Time Management Challenges

Time management, on the surface, appears to be a simple concept. You have tasks and deadlines; the goal is to utilize your time efficiently to meet those deadlines, whether self-imposed or set by others. Yet, despite its apparent simplicity, mastering time management is an uphill battle for many.

A study in the United Kingdom revealed that fewer than 1 in 5 people use any formal time management system. Many rely on scattered email reminders, chaotic day planners, sticky notes, or their own makeshift systems. The internet is teeming with tips, tricks, and hacks to enhance productivity. But the reality is that effectively managing time remains a challenge for most.

For the average person, it's too easy to attribute a string of unproductive days to "one of those weeks" or "the way it is." But poor time management isn't just a fact of life; it's a significant issue costing businesses millions annually and contributing to stress, poor sleep, strained relationships, and burnout among employees. In fact, poor time management practices like procrastination have even been linked to lower incomes.

The Planning Fallacy & Time Management Skills

Strong time management skills aren't inherent for everyone, and even those naturally skilled need to work on keeping those abilities sharp. It's a matter of habits and awareness; mastering time management isn't a quick course but an ongoing process.

While motivation and ambition play a role, it's also a psychological battle, often unnamed. The Planning Fallacy embodies the tendency to underestimate the time required for a project or task, even when past experiences have shown it's unrealistic. This tendency affects our daily lives and the workplace.

For instance, you might allocate an hour or two to write an article, expecting to finish by day's end, even though previous articles took much longer. Recognizing the Planning Fallacy allows you to address it effectively with strategies, tips, and life hacks that enhance time management.

Not Grasping the Real Value of Time

Time, a finite commodity, eludes replenishment. Despite having 8 to 10 work hours daily, an average of 2.5 hours spent on social media diminishes productivity. Recognize the impact of time spent online on work efficiency, echoing the adage, "*One hour of planning can save you 10 hours of doing.*"

Social media isn't the lone challenge; remote and hybrid work blurs work-life boundaries. Effective time managers prioritize tasks, viewing time as a resource for urgent and unplanned activities. Consider not just task duration but its ripple effect on your schedule.

You can Combat the Planning Fallacy with strategies such as:

1. Acknowledge Past Experiences:

   a. Recognize the tendency to underestimate task time.
   b. Awareness is the first step toward overcoming this bias.

2. Break Tasks into Smaller Steps:

   a. Divide tasks into manageable steps for accurate time assessment.
   b. Avoid the trap of underestimating project completion time.

3. Consult with Others:

   a. Seek insights from experienced colleagues or mentors.
   b. Gain valuable perspectives on realistic time expectations.

4. Time Tracking:

    a. Maintain a time log for an eye-opening view of your activities.

    b. Improve time estimates by understanding where your time goes.

5. Set Realistic Deadlines:

    a. Include buffer time for unforeseen issues when setting deadlines.

    b. Enhance the likelihood of meeting deadlines without last-minute rushes.

6. Learn from Past Projects:

    a. Review previous experiences to adjust time estimates.

    b. Use lessons learned to refine future time expectations.

7. Use Time Management Techniques:

    a. Employ methods like the Pomodoro Technique and time blocking.

    b. Create structured approaches to avoid underestimating time.

8. Implement Tools and Apps:

   a. Use time management apps for planning and tracking progress.
   b. Leverage features for setting estimates and deadline reminders.

9. Stay Flexible:

   a. Acknowledge life's unpredictability and be adaptable.
   b. Adjust plans as needed without being too hard on yourself.

10. Reflect & Adjust:

   a. Evaluate task completion time versus initial estimates.
   b. Continuously refine time management skills with this feedback.

Tackling the Planning Fallacy demands patience. As you persistently apply these strategies, knowledge, and strategy become potent weapons in your battle, making you a more accurate time estimator over time.

Life Isn't Static

Imagine this scenario: You've planned your day meticulously, created a to-do list, allocated time blocks, and promised yourself an ultra-productive day. Then, suddenly, your phone buzzes with an urgent work call. Your coworker insists on a last-minute meeting, your child falls ill at school, or you receive a call from the Nobel Prize committee (well, maybe not that last one). But the point is that life throws curveballs our way, and you must be prepared to adapt and adjust your plans.

These unexpected events turn the time management game into a far more complex dynamic optimization problem. It's like trying to navigate a ship through unpredictable waters where the currents can change at any moment. In these situations, maintaining flexibility and quickly re-prioritizing your tasks becomes invaluable.

Here are some strategies to help you navigate life's unpredictable twists and turns:

1. Embrace Flexibility:

    a. Acknowledge the need for adjustments to your initial plan.
    b. Be ready to accommodate urgent matters that may arise.

2. Use Buffer Time:

   a. Build buffer time into your daily schedule.
   b. Allow for addressing unexpected tasks without derailing your entire day.

3. Prioritize on the Fly:

   a. Quickly reassess your task list during unforeseen events.
   b. Prioritize based on urgency and importance for effective response.

4. Delegate Where Possible:

   a. Delegate tasks to team members, coworkers, or family.
   b. Lighten your load during unexpected disruptions.

5. Maintain Clear Communication:

   a. Communicate openly with colleagues, supervisors, and family.
   b. Inform relevant parties promptly when adjusting plans.

6. Resist Overcommitting:

    a. Be cautious about taking on too much in dynamic situations.
    b. Learn to say no to avoid stress and maintain effectiveness.

7. Reflect and Learn:

    a. After navigating unexpected events, reflect on your response.
    b. Learn from experiences to enhance future management of dynamic situations.

Remember, embracing life's dynamic nature and adapting to unexpected events is a hallmark of strong time management. It's not about avoiding disruptions but responding to them with resilience and efficiency. In the ever-changing journey of life, these skills are invaluable.

COMMON TIME WASTERS

Time is a valuable currency, and teenagers, like adults, can often squander it without realizing it. In this section, we'll explore some common time wasters that teenagers might find themselves entangled with.

1. Multitasking:

Teens are notorious for attempting to juggle multiple tasks simultaneously, thinking they're boosting efficiency. For instance, while working on a school project, they might believe it's a great idea to text friends, listen to music, and scroll through social media simultaneously. In reality, multitasking can lead to decreased focus and productivity.

Rather than excelling at multiple tasks, you might find yourself doing everything less effectively. The key to overcoming this time waster is to embrace the power of single-tasking. By dedicating your focus to one task at a time, you'll complete it more efficiently, freeing up time for other activities.

2. Unnecessary Meetings:

Teens can also get trapped in the cycle of unnecessary meetings. Whether it's group projects at school or social gatherings, sometimes "meetings" become an excuse to hang out with friends rather than focusing on the task at hand.

To address this time waster, you can utilize time blocking. Set aside specific periods for concentrated work, and let your friends know you're unavailable during those times. By doing this, you minimize interruptions and maximize productivity.

3. Social Media/Online Distractions:

Social media and online distractions can be an enormous time sink for teenagers. Scrolling through Instagram, watching TikTok videos, or diving into endless YouTube rabbit holes are common culprits.

The key to combating this time waster is setting boundaries. Designate specific times for indulging in your favorite online activities. When studying or working on a project, consider using website blockers or apps that help you stay focused. These tools can restrict access to time-draining websites, ensuring your focus remains intact.

4. Too Much Gossiping:

Teenagers sometimes find themselves caught up in gossip and idle chatter. Instead of discussing important matters, they may end up chatting about trivial or irrelevant topics, which can consume precious hours.

This phenomenon is not so different from adults having chatty coworkers who disrupt their concentration. One strategy to counteract excessive chatting is time blocking. Dedicate specific time slots for your work or study sessions and make it clear to friends that you're unavailable during those hours. This approach minimizes interruptions and helps you maintain your focus and productivity.

5. Can't Say No:

Many teenagers struggle with the inability to decline additional commitments. Whether it's taking on more school projects or agreeing to more social outings, an inability to say no can lead to overcommitment and heightened stress.

To combat this time waster, remember that it's okay to decline politely. Prioritize your existing responsibilities and maintain your well-being. Learning to say no empowers you to manage your time more effectively.

Each of these time wasters has unique strategies to over-come, often involving setting boundaries and practicing self-discipline. Remember, the more effectively you tackle these time wasters, the more time you'll have to dedicate to what truly matters in your life. Time is your most valuable resource—use it wisely.

2

THE POWER OF A STUDY SPACE

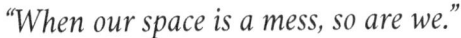

"When our space is a mess, so are we."

— LIBBY SANDER, HARVARD BUSINESS REVIEW

As a kid, I had a corner of my room dedicated to being my study area. I would make a mess out of my room all day, but that corner remained spotless. There would be clothes on the bed, a towel on the chair, and a basketball on the floor, but my study area remained clear. My parents were quite strict about it, always telling me to keep my study separate. It used to bug me at times, though – if it's so important, why don't they just dedicate a separate room for me to study?

Of course, being a teenager, I didn't always listen. My parents would clear the area themselves if they ever saw clutter in that corner. Of course, this meant I always had a clean, organized area to focus on my studies.

As I grew older, I started to understand the wisdom behind their insistence. That small, uncluttered space became my sanctuary, a place where I could immerse myself in my studies without distractions. It made me realize that a dedicated study space isn't just about neatness; it's about the psychology of learning.

WHY YOUR STUDY SPACE MATTERS

The impact of your study environment is more profound than you might think. It's not just about having a clean desk or proper lighting. It's about the mental space it creates. A well-designed study space isn't a luxury but a necessity. It sets the stage for focused learning, helping you concentrate, minimize distractions, and boost productivity.

When you settle into your designated study area, it signals to your brain that it's time to work, creating a clear boundary between leisure and study. The presence of that dedicated space says, "*This is where I learn. This is where I achieve my goals.*"

But you might still wonder, "*Why not study in my bed or at the kitchen table?*" These spaces can serve short-term needs but often hinder deep, uninterrupted work.

Think about it – even something as simple as choosing between typing on a laptop while lounging on a couch versus sitting upright at a table can impact your productivity. The latter can increase your typing speed and reduce errors, helping you work more efficiently. It's all part of the psychology of productivity.

Can You Study Anywhere?

Imagine a painter without a blank canvas, a chef without a kitchen, or an author without a blank page. Just as artists need the right space and tools to create, students require a dedicated study space to learn effectively.

When you settle into your designated study area, it's like a signal to your brain that it's time to work. This simple act creates a clear boundary between leisure and study, allowing your mind to shift into learning mode. The presence of that dedicated space says, "*This is where I learn. This is where I achieve my goals.*"

The Kitchen Table

The kitchen table is a familiar and often-used study space, particularly for students. For many, it offers a convenient and communal place to work on assignments while amid family activities. Before I had that dedicated study space, the kitchen table served as my after-school homework hub—a place where I could spread out my books and assignments. My mom would be cooking dinner while keeping an eye on my progress.

However, while the kitchen table might be an acceptable spot for doing homework or short-term work, it's essential to understand its limitations, especially for extended study sessions. Here's why it's not the ideal choice for an efficient study space:

- *Distractions*: The bustling kitchen, filled with enticing smells and family chatter, poses challenges for concentrated tasks like reading or essay writing.
- *Noise*: Blenders and dishwashers contribute to a noisy kitchen environment, hindering clear thinking and focus.
- *Lack of Privacy*: While the kitchen fosters family togetherness, it may lack the privacy required for tasks like online exams or sensitive assignments.
- *Physical Space*: Depending on its size, the kitchen might not offer ample space for the comfortable spreading of materials, leading to potential clutter and inefficiency.
- *Timed Activities*: Suited for activities with breaks, the kitchen table may not support the sustained focus needed for extended study sessions.

While the kitchen table can be an excellent place for younger students who need immediate parental support and a balance between learning and daily activities, it might not be the best choice for older you if you are tackling more complex assignments that demand uninterrupted focus.

The Bed: The Illusion of Comfort

Ah, the bed – a place of rest, relaxation, and sometimes, illusory comfort. For many, the allure of studying in cozy blankets and plush pillows can be tempting, especially when seeking a change of scenery. As a teenager, I occasionally gave in to this temptation, thinking, "*What could be better than studying while comfortably nestled in my bed?*" This was particularly true during the peak winter season.

At first glance, the bed seems like an inviting study spot. It offers immediate comfort, like a gentle hug from your favorite teddy bear. But beneath this allure lies a web of productivity pitfalls that can turn your study session into a catnap waiting to happen.

Here's why the bed's promise of comfort often turns out to be an illusion:

1. *Blurring the Lines*: When you decide to study on your bed, you're also sending a signal to your brain that it's time for relaxation. This mental association can lead to a lack of focus and productivity. Your bed should be reserved for rest, not rigorous mental tasks. It's akin to trying to

swim in a bathtub – you'll be restricted, uncomfortable, and ultimately inefficient.

2. *The Temptation of Rest*: Your bed is designed for rest and rejuvenation, making it a place of utmost comfort. As a result, it's easy to give in to the temptation to take a nap, watch a TV show, or scroll through social media instead of hitting the books. Studying here is like sailing in treacherous waters; the siren song of leisure and procrastination lures you in.

3. *Physical Discomfort*: Surprisingly, the bed, despite its soft exterior, can be physically uncomfortable for studying. The absence of proper lumbar support, inadequate space for materials, and often improper posture can lead to discomfort, back pain, and even headaches. Your once-comfy bed can quickly transform into a place of discomfort and distraction.

4. *Fragmented Focus*: The relaxed atmosphere of your bed can result in fragmented focus. It's challenging to maintain continuous attention when you're comfortably reclined. Your mind can easily drift to unrelated thoughts, and you'll find yourself reading the same sentence multiple times.

5. *Limited Workspace*: Beds aren't designed for work. You'll often find a lack of adequate space to spread out textbooks, notebooks, or a computer comfortably. The limited surface area can force

you into awkward positions, further contributing to physical discomfort and inefficiency.

The paradox of the bed as a study space lies in its initial appeal – it feels like a retreat from the demands of traditional study environments. But, over time, you'll realize it's a trap, pulling you into a world of sluggishness and diminished productivity. For the brief moments of surface-level comfort, you pay the price of lost time, subpar study sessions, and perhaps even the nagging feeling that you should be doing something more worthwhile.

In hindsight, my younger self's occasional resistance to my parents' insistence on a dedicated study space made perfect sense. The bed, while charming, had a knack for blurring the line between work and leisure, leaving my productivity in a state of slumber. As I matured, I came to recognize that a dedicated study area was indispensable for efficient and effective studying.

Your Dedicated Study Space: A Mental Commitment

A dedicated study space, on the other hand, provides an environment that promotes discipline, consistency, and routine. It's a physical commitment to your education. When you sit at your desk or work table, your brain knows it's time to concentrate. This consistent association between your study space and focused learning enhances your ability to stay on task and remain productive.

In your dedicated study space, the distractions are minimized. It's your haven for learning, free from the temptations of leisure. This separation is crucial for maintaining a balance between work and play. As you advance through your academic journey, this practice becomes invaluable in your future career. Your work desk at home now will eventually transform into your office desk or workstation in the professional world.

The bottom line is that the space where you study matters, and it's about more than just having a clean and organized desk. It's about creating an environment that supports learning, enhances productivity, and, most importantly, helps you reach your educational goals. Your workspace is a vital resource for your academic success; the key is discovering what works for you. It begins with finding yourself a suitable space for study.

STUDY SPACE COMPARISON – A QUICK SUMMARY

A well-designed study space isn't a luxury; it's a necessity. It sets the stage for focused learning, helping you concentrate, minimize distractions, and boost productivity. When you settle into your designated study area, it signals to your brain that it's time to work, creating a clear boundary between leisure and study.

Here is a comparison between different study places that you might be tempted to choose:

Study Area	Distractions	Noise Level	Privacy	Comfort	Space
Bed	Moderate	Low	Low	High	Limited
Kitchen Table	High	High	Low	Moderate	Limited
Library	Low	Low	High	Moderate	Ample
Friend's Home	High	Moderate	Variable	Variable	Variable
Dedicated Study Space	Low	Low	High	Variable	Moderate to High

The dedicated study space stands out as a preferable option with low distractions, low noise levels, high privacy, adjustable comfort, and moderate to ample space. It provides an environment that fosters productivity, concentration, and a clear separation between leisure and study.

HOW TO CREATE A FOCUS-FRIENDLY WORKSPACE

Your study space's effectiveness is not solely defined by its location but also by its elements. A conducive workspace can significantly impact your productivity and overall learning experience. You need:

1. *Comfortable Seating:* Your study journey deserves an ergonomic chair providing lumbar support and

adjustable settings for enduring comfort during long hours.

2. *Adequate Space:* Like a treasure map on a postage stamp, a cluttered desk is a jungle. Choose spaciousness to promote focus—spread out study materials comfortably.

3. *Good Lighting:* Your guiding light in the academic seascape, prefer natural light or bright LED bulbs strategically placed to minimize shadows..

4. *Desk:* Your academic crow's nest, choose a roomy, sturdy desk to withstand the storms of study— chart your course, scribe essays, and bring mathematical mysteries to life.

5. *Source of Power:* An adventurer needs energy— ensure your workspace offers easy access to power outlets, with a surge protector as your fortress.

6. *Water Bottle:* In the sea of knowledge, hydration is your lifeboat—keep a water bottle on hand to quench your thirst and keep brain waves flowing

7. *Desk Organizers:* Maintain order in your academic waters with organizers, preventing study treasures from vanishing into the abyss.

8. *Personal Diary/Paper Planner:* A diary is your treasure map for time management. Track your quests, deadlines, and appointments, ensuring you navigate the academic waters with precision.

This reminds me, *why did the student bring a ladder to their study space?* Because they wanted to go to a higher level of learning! But remember, it's not about the height; it's about having the right elements. Having the right ladder is essential to ensure that you reach the intended height and that it doesn't break halfway! Similarly, you need a comfy chair, a spacious desk, and good lighting that elevate your study experience and won't abandon you when you need them most (*this is experience talking*).

I distinctly remember sitting down to study with a hand-me-down chair. By the time I found the perfect spot, I realized I'd run out of power for my laptop. As I reached for my charger, I knocked over a pile of pens, spilling ink all over my notes. Between this chaos, I tried to plan my study schedule in my head but soon realized I was lost without my trusty diary, now spoiled with ink!

WHAT ARE DISTRACTIONS? THINGS THAT MIGHT SEEM PRODUCTIVE BUT AREN'T

You might be surprised to find out that many things that appear to enhance productivity can, in reality, be major distractions. Let's take a look at some of these deceptive elements in your study space:

Television (or Source of "White Noise")

While some consider TV or "white noise" background soothing, it often turns into a distracting storm. A sitcom laugh or interesting news can pull focus, making navigating your studies challenging. Imagine sailing to study but getting caught in a whirlpool of entertainment.

Music with Lyrics

Music can be a study companion, but lyrics can lead you off course. Choose instrumental or ambient tracks to stay on track without getting lost in the song's words. Just as scientists don't trust atoms because they make up everything, lyrics can fill your thoughts when you should be studying.

Smartphone (Even If You're Not Using It)

The smartphone, often a study buddy, can quickly become a digital prankster. Its mere presence tempts you into social media, scrolling or texting friends, hijacking your educational quest. It's like having a treasure chest with a tempting lock you're not supposed to open while studying.

Taking Frequent, Random Breaks (& Not Timing Them)

Spontaneous breaks may feel liberating, but they often stretch longer than you realize, reducing overall productivity. Embrace the Rule of 52 and 17: Work for 52 minutes, then enjoy a 17-minute break. This structured approach guides your study journey like a compass, preventing the express route to procrastination ville.

BONUS: FEATURELESS WALLS/SPACES

The belief that featureless, minimalist study spaces are conducive to productivity is a common one. Many think that fewer visual distractions equal better focus. However, this idea might not hold up to scrutiny.

Research has shown that having a window with a view, especially a green one, can enhance your performance and concentration. In a 1978 experiment, participants with a window view outperformed those with no view, showing that nature's beauty can work wonders for your study space. It's like choosing between a plain treasure chest and one adorned with carvings – the latter holds the real treasure for your focus.

Your study space should be a fortress of focus, and that means eliminating these deceptive distractions. As you continue to fine-tune your space for optimal productivity, remember that not everything that glitters is gold – and not every so-called productivity enhancer lives up to the hype. Stay mindful of these potential traps and create a study environment supporting your goals.

THE IMPORTANCE OF DECLUTTERING

A cluttered study space might seem like a cozy, lived-in environment, but in reality, it's a productivity killer. Think of clutter as the lurking sea monster beneath the surface, waiting to capsize your academic voyage. It's not just about aesthetics; it significantly impacts your focus and time management.

Handy Hacks for a Clutter-Free Space

Imagine you're on a quest to declutter your desk and need a reliable guide. Well, here's your map: the *Decluttering Formula*. This formula incorporates five key factors to help you decide what stays and what goes. Let me illustrate how it works with a real-life example.

- **Recency:** Consider how recently you've used an item. If it's been gathering dust for months, it's probably time to part ways.
- **Frequency:** Think about how often you use the item. Frequent-use items earn their place, while rarely-used items might need to sail away.
- **Acquisition Cost:** Reflect on how much the item cost you. The value of an item doesn't always lie in

its price, but this factor helps you evaluate its importance.

- **Storage Cost:** Ponder the space it occupies. Valuable desk real estate shouldn't be wasted on items that can find a home elsewhere.
- **Retrieval Cost:** Contemplate the ease of finding the item when needed. If it takes a treasure hunt every time, it's probably not worth keeping.

I once applied this formula to my own cluttered desk. My desk was a chaotic treasure chest of stationery, old notes, and knick-knacks. One day (while I was admittedly grounded), I realized that:

- Some of the items had been untouched for years (Recency).
- Others I rarely used (Frequency).
- A few were expensive but not useful for my studies (Acquisition Cost).
- The storage they occupied hindered my workspace organization (Storage Cost) and
- Finding them when I needed them was like navigating a maze (Retrieval Cost).

With this formula in hand, I started clearing everything, classifying my things, and arranging them *away* from my study space. The result? A desk that was a haven of focus and productivity.

ALLOCATE DECLUTTERING TIME

Decluttering your workspace doesn't have to be a daunting task you tackle once every few months (or, like me, when you're grounded). Instead, you should integrate it into your daily or weekly routine for better management.

If daily sessions don't suit your schedule, dedicate one hour weekly to thorough decluttering. Choose a specific day, like Sunday, for a stress-free weekly cleanup.

Ensure your desk serves its purpose – a dedicated workspace, not a storage unit. Store books on shelves, bags in closets, and snacks in the kitchen. This maintains a tidy environment, minimizing distractions and optimizing your study sessions.

Key practices to maintain should be:

- **Daily 15-Minute Sessions**: Clear clutter and organize materials.
- **Weekly One-Hour Declutter**: Thoroughly tidy up for a stress-free environment.
- **Organized Book Storage**: Designate shelves for study materials.
- **Bag-Free Desk**: Keep bags stored in closets to free up valuable desk space.
- **Kitchen Snacks**: Avoid desk clutter by storing snacks in the kitchen.

These storage practices help ensure that your desk remains clutter-free and you focus on productive study sessions.

Give Away/Throw Away One Item Every Week

Decluttering is more than just eliminating items; it's an opportunity to be mindful of what you keep. Challenge yourself to give away or throw away one item every week. While some sources suggest a daily approach, adapting it to your desk environment can be highly effective.

My mother made me embrace the "one item a week" decluttering practice as an alternative to daily decluttering. If I didn't do it on my own, she'd just pick something up randomly and hide it (she wouldn't throw it out right away as she wasn't always sure what was important and what wasn't). If I started throwing a fit trying to find it and explained how important it was, I would have to trade it back with her.

This approach proved to be a manageable and sustainable way to keep my desk pristine. It allowed me to carefully evaluate each item before parting with it. Each week, I consciously chose what needed to leave my workspace, ensuring a gradual yet significant transformation of my desk's cleanliness. And in hindsight, I believe it saved me from becoming a hoarder, too!

This approach prevents clutter from accumulating on your desk and helps you assess the usefulness of items more thoughtfully.

Is It Useful & Does It Spark Joy?

The KonMari method, popularized by Marie Kondo, centers around one fundamental question: "*Does it spark joy?*" Apply this philosophy to your desk items. Suppose an item no longer serves a practical purpose or fails to evoke positivity. In that case, it's a sign that it might be time to say goodbye. Here's how this method can work for your study space:

Applying the "usefulness" and "joy" filters allows you to maintain a clean, personal, organized study space that fosters focus and productivity.

Regularly Review Decorations

Decorations can add a personal touch to your study space, but moderation is key. Periodically reviewing your desk decorations ensures they don't take over your workspace. Here's how you can strike the right balance:

I once adorned my desk with various decorations, believing they would enhance my study environment. This is also why I mentioned above that the throw-away rule saved me from becoming a hoarder.

Over time, I realized many of these decorations had started to distract rather than inspire. By conducting a periodic review, I could maintain a balance between personalization and functionality. I kept the items that enhanced my study experience and bid farewell to those that no longer had a purpose.

Remember, *your study space should be a place of focus*. While decorations are acceptable, their presence should never hinder your productivity. Regularly assessing your decorations ensures your workspace remains an oasis of efficiency.

TRACKING YOUR DESK'S METAMORPHOSIS

Now that you've been equipped with the wisdom and tools to declutter your study space, it's time to start your own personal odyssey toward a neater, more organized, and clutter-free desk.

Like any great quest, this journey might take a few hours or even several days, depending on your pace. Remember, there's no rush; *the key is to do it right, not necessarily fast.*

Step 1: The "Before" Photo/Video

- Take a "before" photo or video of your current workspace to kick off your transformation.

- This is your starting point, the snapshot of the cluttered seas you're about to navigate. Trust me; you'll want to remember this moment.

Step 2: The Transformation Process

- As you dive into the process, consider filming your journey. Document your experiences, struggles, and triumphant moments as you implement the decluttering strategies laid out in this chapter.
- Share your story, and remember that your pace is unique—there's no need to rush.

Step 3: The "After" Photo/Video

- Once you've conquered the chaos, take a triumphant "after" photo or video. This represents your successful voyage to an organized and pristine workspace. Behold the transformation!

Step 4: Display the Results

- Now, don't just tuck these visuals away. Find a prominent place to display the "before" and "after" images.

Pin them on a corkboard, attach them to your fridge, or even compile them into a video or a reel. These visuals will constantly remind you what your study space can become, inspiring you to keep it clutter-free.

As you clear your study space and understand its significance, you will find yourself ready for more opportunities. Your learning experiences will further empower these opportunities, foster productivity, and set the stage for educational and personal triumphs. It also sets the stage for a more streamlined future as you grow up. Like a well-organized study space, the chapter has provided the structure and tools you need to unlock your full potential.

But remember, this is not the end of your journey; *it's just one leg of the adventure.* Next, we'll take a closer look at some other key elements you need to manage yourself and your time better for a lasting and successful future.

3

THE POWER OF A PLANNER

 "By failing to plan, you are preparing to fail."

— BENJAMIN FRANKLIN

I remember my father's unwavering commitment to his trusty planner during my teen years. It wasn't one of those sleek, digital calendars on a smartphone nowadays that nags you with incessant notifications.

No, it was a large, imposing physical planner with sturdy covers, thick pages, and an air of authority. My father managed to fill that planner to the brim with notes, to-dos, and appointments. He was the epitome of dedication when it came to planning, and once something found its place on those pages, there was no changing it. *It. Had. To. Be. Done.*

In an era when digital calendars and planners have become the norm, my father's preference for the physical planner seemed almost nostalgic. He had an uncanny ability to maintain a structured day, a quality I only came to appreciate fully as I grew older.

In a world where reminders pop up on our screens at every turn, there's a certain elegance in having a planner that doesn't badger you with constant notifications, a tool you can choose to turn off if you need a break.

In this chapter, we will explore the power of a physical planner in an age of digital distractions. We'll look into the benefits of this underrated tool and learn how effective planning can transform your life.

THE PHYSICAL PLANNER: AN UNDERRATED TOOL

Today, the charm of a physical paper planner often goes unnoticed. Yet, there's a profound case to be made for this old-school method of organization. It is, in essence, a critical part of what will make you a time management guru - an example for all those around. Let's explore why a paper planner, as opposed to its digital counterpart, is crucial in helping us stay organized, productive, and in control of our lives.

Stronger Memory Recall

The age-old practice of jotting notes with pen and paper has proven to be more than just nostalgic; it offers tangible cognitive benefits. In a 2021 study, participants who embraced analog note-taking experienced heightened brain activity and superior memory compared to their digital counterparts. Remarkably, the handwritten note-takers completed their tasks 25 percent faster.

The physical act of writing on paper provides a unique cognitive advantage that digital tools struggle to emulate. University of Tokyo neuroscience professor Kuniyoshi L. Sakai, a study author, emphasized that the paper offers distinctive information for robust memory recall, making handwritten notes more effective.

Despite the digital era's prevalence, the tactile connection between paper and pen fosters concentration, focus, and a personal connection unmatched by electronic devices. Professor Sakai's insight supports the idea that the distinctive qualities of pen and paper contribute to memory enhancement.

During my high school years, my best friend was the embodiment of chaos when it came to his schedule. He was notorious for double-booking himself, forgetting birthdays, and missing important appointments. It wasn't until he came home one night for dinner and saw my father jotting things down that he decided to give a paper planner a shot. Coincidentally, college was about to start soon, too, so it was truly a "new beginning" for him.

At first, he was skeptical, of course. However, we all soon realized the transformative effect of this age-old tool. It took him a while to understand the difference, though. He only saw the difference in himself when someone at a college party complimented him on *actually being there.*

From then on, he started penning down her daily tasks, assignments, and social commitments. It was a visual representation of his life, something he could touch, feel, and annotate. To his surprise, his memory also seemed sharper as a result. He no longer scrambled to recall the due dates of his assignments, calling us in the middle of the night to confirm. It was all neatly laid out in his trusty planner.

Frees Up Active Working Memory

Imagine your working memory as a mental workspace. It's the place where you temporarily hold information while thinking or solving problems. However, this workspace is limited, and when it's overloaded, it can hinder your ability to focus and think clearly.

Here's where the paper planner comes to the rescue. It acts as a scaffold, helping you offload some of the information from your working memory onto paper. For instance, visual planning sheets can organize your thoughts for writing, equations can aid your problem-solving in math, and note cards can store quotations.

Writing these down on paper frees up space in your active working memory, allowing you to think more deeply and efficiently.

Cools Brain on Stressful Tasks

Studies suggest that the act of writing can be a calming influence when faced with stressful tasks. It's like a mental exhale. Writing down your to-dos or appointments in a planner creates a sense of control and structure, reducing the cognitive burden these tasks might have on your brain.

When the world feels chaotic, a physical planner can be a calming sanctuary where you can sort your thoughts, plan your day, and regain a sense of order. This psychological relief can be particularly helpful when facing challenging or stressful tasks.

Less Tech Usage

One of the often-overlooked benefits of a paper planner is its ability to keep you tech-free, at least for a while. In a world where smartphones are practically an extension of our hands, using a paper planner allows you to start your day without the screen time. It's a refreshing break from the constant notifications and digital distractions that can dominate our mornings.

A paper planner lets you kickstart your day with intention and mindfulness rather than immediately plunging into the digital whirlpool.

Less Digital Distractions

Now, let's talk about those notorious "mini-distractions." You know them well. They're the constant pings, dings, and notifications that sneak into your day, diverting your attention from what matters. The digital world is rife with these tiny time thieves.

A paper planner, on the other hand, offers a respite from these distractions. When writing in your planner, you're in your own world. No pop-up messages or news alerts. You're free to focus on your thoughts, tasks, and goals without being constantly pulled in different directions.

Improves Your Planning Quality

To understand the impact of paper planning on the quality of your plans, let's look at the findings from Columbia Business School's research. In three separate experiments involving over 1,079 people, they discovered that individuals who used paper calendars developed higher-quality plans and had a significantly higher success rate in fulfilling them compared to digital users.

In fact, paper calendar users completed 53% of their plans, while digital users lagged behind at 33%. The key takeaway was that paper planning provides a visual record of your accomplishments, fueling your sense of accomplishment. It also helps you evaluate your workload, identify where your time has gone, and gain insights into approaching tasks more efficiently moving forward.

There's a story I told my daughter once about this, which would fit great here. There was once a young chef named Mia. She dreamed of opening her own restaurant, and her physical planner was the secret ingredient to her success.

While her peers opted for digital tools, Mia clung to her traditional planner, filling its pages with daily goals, weekly specials, and shopping lists. Despite initial jests from colleagues, Mia's commitment to her paper planner bore fruit.

As months passed, Mia's restaurant soared to success, lauded for its flawless dishes and inviting atmosphere. Friends marveled at her achievements, prompting one to inquire about her seemingly effortless management.

With a smile, Mia unveiled her planner—a vibrant mosaic of tabs, comments, and checkmarks. *"This is my recipe for success,"* she asserted. *"It's not merely about planning; it's about creating something tangible that helps me stay on top of things and see the bigger picture."*

In a world overflowing with digital options, a paper planner may seem like a relic from a bygone era. Yet, its simplicity and effectiveness in improving memory, reducing working memory load, and decreasing stress make it a powerful tool.

EFFECTIVE PLANNING WITH YOUR PHYSICAL PLANNER

When it comes to making the most out of your physical planner, a few questions come to mind first. Why is a planner necessary in the first place? Why invest time and effort in crafting a meticulous schedule when digital alternatives are at our fingertips?

A planner serves as more than just a tool; it's a gateway to structured living. In an era marked by the frantic pace of life, where tasks and commitments abound, a planner provides a stable foundation. It's a reliable companion in an unpredictable world, offering a sense of order and purpose.

When we don't plan, we subject ourselves to chaos. Without a planner, we rely on our memory, which, as we've discussed, can be unreliable, leading to forgotten tasks and missed opportunities. A planner becomes the custodian of your commitments, guarding them against the forgetfulness of your mind and the chaos of daily life.

Students, in particular, stand to gain significantly from planning their weeks. Academic life is a juggling act, requiring students to balance classes, assignments, exams, and social activities. Without a plan, they may find themselves overwhelmed and floundering.

Planning provides students with a roadmap for their week. It not only ensures that they don't miss important classes or assignment deadlines but also creates opportunities for personal growth and relaxation. With a well-structured schedule, students can allocate time for studying, attending classes, and pursuing their passions. It's like having a secret ally in the battle against forgetfulness – a bit like your personal planner is the superhero cape your memory wears.

Benefits of Planning Ahead

Planning ahead is more than just an organizational habit; it's a lifestyle choice. It's the difference between drifting aimlessly and progressing with purpose. The benefits of planning ahead are numerous and extend into every aspect of life.

- **Time Management**: Planning optimizes time usage by prioritizing tasks and reducing stress associated with time constraints.
- **Goal Achievement**: Planning serves as the roadmap to goal attainment, aligning each step

with the ultimate objective, whether academic, professional, or personal.

- **Reduced Procrastination**: Setting specific task schedules through planning creates commitment, acting as a potent deterrent against procrastination.
- **Enhanced Productivity**: Organized planning minimizes decision-making time, fostering efficient task execution and transforming each moment into progress.
- **Stress Reduction**: Planning alleviates stress by eliminating the anxiety of forgetting tasks, providing a sense of control over life's uncertainties.
- **Adaptability**: Effective planning cultivates adaptability, acting as a compass in navigating unexpected changes while maintaining focus on overarching goals.

Planning To Achieve Specific Goals

To understand how planning helps students reach their goals, let's revisit the findings from the earlier section. According to the Columbia Business School's research, individuals who use paper calendars develop higher quality plans and have a significantly higher success rate in fulfilling them.

When we extrapolate this to the context of students, it's evident that effective planning can make the difference between academic excellence and mediocrity. Paper planning, unlike digital options, allows students to craft more detailed and cohesive plans. It helps them account for how scheduled events interact or impact each other. In essence, it empowers them to plan ahead, a skill that's indispensable in the academic journey.

One of the frameworks that can immensely aid students in goal setting and achievement is the *SMART Goals framework*.

WHAT ARE SMART GOALS?

SMART is an acronym that stands for Specific, Measurable, Achievable, Relevant, and Time-bound. Let's break down each element:

- **Specific**: Goals should be unambiguous. A specific goal answers the questions: What do you want to accomplish? Why is it essential? How will you achieve it?
- **Measurable**: Goals should be quantifiable. Measuring progress provides motivation and a clear indicator of whether you've achieved the goal. Questions to consider include: How will you track your progress? How will you know when you've reached your goal?

- **Achievable**: While it's important to aim high, goals should also be attainable. You should have the skills and resources necessary to accomplish the goal. Consider what's needed to reach the goal and whether it's realistic.
- **Relevant**: Goals should align with your values, interests, and objectives. A relevant goal is meaningful and contributes to your overall development.
- **Time-Bound**: Every goal should have a deadline. It adds urgency and prevents procrastination. Set a specific timeframe within which you aim to achieve the goal.

Applying the SMART framework to goal setting significantly increases the likelihood of fulfillment. It transforms vague aspirations into actionable plans. For instance, instead of setting a broad goal like "*Improve grades*," a student could set a SMART goal: "*Raise my chemistry grade from a B to an A in the next semester by attending extra tutorials, practicing problems daily, and seeking help when needed.*"

It's like turning a nebulous dream into a treasure map – *X marks the A!*

By breaking down a goal using the SMART criteria, students gain clarity and focus. They have a clear direction, a means of tracking progress, and a deadline that creates a sense of urgency.

A HOW-TO: TRANSFORMING YOUR PLANNER INTO A GOAL ACHIEVEMENT MACHINE

Effective planning is not merely about jotting down tasks and deadlines; it's a dynamic process that takes you from dreams to tangible accomplishments. This "How-To" section will walk you through the steps to transform your planner into a goal-achievement machine.

Step 1: Decide What Type of Planner Suits Your Needs

Before diving into the nitty-gritty of planning, let's start with the basics. Just as every person is unique, so are their planning needs. You wouldn't try to fit a square peg into a round hole. Likewise, your planner should cater to your individual preferences. Take a moment to consider what type of planner suits you best.

Would you prefer a big calendar-type planner that sits at your desk and provides ample space for writing, or is a portable version more your style?

Do you like the convenience of pages with printed templates, or are you the creative type who'd thrive with a blank journal featuring simple grid pages?

Your planner is your blank page; its design should align with your planning personality.

Step 2: Think About Your Week in Advance

Effective planning begins by getting ahead of the game. Take a spare piece of paper and jot down everything that needs to be accomplished during the upcoming week. This initial brainstorming session serves as a blueprint for your planner. It ensures that no crucial tasks or events slip through the cracks.

By starting with this overview, you set the stage for a successful planning process, ensuring that nothing is forgotten or overlooked.

Step 3: Differentiate Between Events and To-Do Lists

One critical aspect of effective planning is distinguishing between events and to-do lists. Events are fixed appointments or commitments that have a specific time and date. On the other hand, to-do lists consist of tasks that need to be accomplished but do not have a set time or date associated with them.

This differentiation between events and to-do lists is crucial for maintaining clarity in your planner. It allows you to see at a glance what your schedule looks like and where you have room for additional tasks or activities.

Step 4: Be Realistic

Effective planning hinges on being realistic about what you can achieve within a given day. While enthusiasm is admirable, setting unrealistic expectations for your day can lead to frustration and burnout.

Consider your personal limits and how you function best. Remember that breaks and downtime are essential for maintaining productivity and well-being. Your planner should reflect a balanced approach that accommodates your commitments and leaves room for self-care and relaxation.

Step 5: Break Down Large Projects Into Smaller Tasks

Large projects can be daunting but become manageable when broken down into smaller, more achievable tasks. Your planner is an excellent tool for this purpose.

For instance, if your goal is to complete a research paper, you can allocate different sections of the paper to specific days or weeks. This systematic approach ensures that you make steady progress and prevents the overwhelming feeling of tackling a colossal project.

Step 6: Plan for Fun/Leisure Time As Well

Planning isn't solely about work and responsibilities; it's also about enhancing your quality of life. Make sure to allocate time in your planner for leisure activities and fun. Whether it's spending time with loved ones, pursuing a hobby, or simply enjoying a good book, these moments of joy and relaxation are equally vital.

Your planner can help you strike a balance between your work and personal life, promoting holistic well-being.

Step 7: Be Flexible

Life is unpredictable, and sometimes, despite the best-laid plans, unexpected events can disrupt your schedule. Embrace the spirit of flexibility in your planner. When changes occur, don't view them as failures but as opportunities to adapt.

Your planner is your guide, but it should also be adaptable. If a task can't be completed on a particular day, reschedule it without guilt. Being flexible is a key aspect of maintaining a positive planning experience.

THE POWER OF PLANNING: BRINGING DREAMS TO LIFE

Planning can seem like a mundane task in the frenzied pace of modern life. However, as we've explored in this chapter, planning is far from dull. It's the compass that guides you toward your dreams, the sentinel that guards your commitments, and the architect of your achievements.

Your physical planner is more than a book of pages; it's a book of dreams. From better memory recall to reduced stress and improved productivity, your planner offers an array of benefits that extend into every aspect of your life.

A Tale of Transformation For Better Life Skills

As I grew up with my father's unwavering commitment to his trusty planner, I wasn't the only one in our family influenced by this dedication. My younger brother, Alex, was somewhat of a teenage rebel during his earlier years. He was notorious for last-minute cramming, missed appointments, and general disorganization.

His room was the perfect reflection of his chaotic life – books scattered on the floor, laundry piled high, and a desk buried under a sea of papers. Yet, I witnessed a remarkable transformation as he transitioned into his late teens.

One clear memory that stands out is from his high school graduation day. You see, in his earlier years, the concept of planning was alien to him. But as he approached graduation, the reality of life beyond high school began to sink in. He realized that organizing his responsibilities was key to navigating the transition into adulthood. It was a turning point, and I was fortunate enough to witness it.

Once a chaotic battlefield, Alex's room slowly transformed into order and productivity. One day, as I walked into his room to ask him a question, I couldn't help but notice the changes.

His desk, which used to be a paper vortex, was now neatly organized. There was a calendar on the wall with color-coded entries, and his planner sat open, displaying a week's worth of carefully outlined tasks. Of course, this wasn't a one-day twist. I saw all this unfold slowly over the course of a few days.

I asked him what had brought about this transformation. He grinned and pointed at a section of his planner. *"This,"* he said, tapping his finger on a specific day. *"I saw Dad planning once and decided to give it a shot for this event. And well, it worked. One of the best days of my life, this."*

It was a powerful moment. He explained how he'd decided to take control of his life and make the most of his time. His planner had become his best friend, guiding him through the sea of deadlines and commitments. But there was one anecdote that truly highlighted the effectiveness of this new approach.

A couple of months later, I overheard Alex talking on the phone. He was discussing a group project for college with his classmates. They were all sharing ideas on how to approach the assignment. As I eavesdropped (*a little guiltily, I admit*), I couldn't help but notice his calm and authoritative tone.

He was explaining a detailed plan, breaking down the project into tasks, assigning roles to each member, and setting deadlines. His classmates seemed impressed, and they readily agreed to the plan. Once he hung up, I had to inquire about his newfound leadership skills.

He chuckled and told me that planning wasn't just about managing his time but also about managing teamwork. He realized that effective planning was an invaluable skill for collaborative projects. It ensured that everyone was on the same page, knew their responsibilities, and promptly met deadlines.

In that moment, I saw my younger brother's transformation into a more organized and effective individual, and I couldn't help but be proud. He had embraced the power of planning, just as our father had, and it was changing the course of his life.

I watched Alex go from being a rebel teenager to a responsible adult, and it was evident that the lessons he had learned from our father's devotion to planning had played a significant role in this remarkable change.

It was a beautiful example of how the little things our father did every day had a lasting impact on how we managed our lives. The planner had become more than just a tool; it was a symbol of transformation and growth, a reminder that with the right mindset and planning, we could achieve anything we set our minds to.

This shows that your physical planner is more than a book of pages; it's a book of dreams. It's a blank page upon which you paint your goals, and with each stroke of planning, you bring those dreams closer to reality. From better memory recall to reduced stress and improved productivity, your planner offers an array of benefits that extend into every aspect of your life.

By applying effective planning techniques and adopting the SMART Goals framework, you can transform your planner into a goal-achievement machine. You can set clear objectives, break them down into manageable tasks, and systematically work toward your dreams. Your planner will be your partner in this journey, a reliable companion ensuring you stay on track.

4

TIME MANAGEMENT TECHNIQUES

"Time management is an oxymoron. Time is beyond our control, and the clock keeps ticking regardless of how we lead our lives. Priority management is the answer to maximizing the time we have."

— JOHN C. MAXWELL

The majority of people don't use a dedicated time management system. 82% have been reported to just *"wing it."* A to-do list doesn't count (even though 33% rely on them to manage work). Having a planner may feel like it's just something extra to do in your otherwise busy day. However, studies have shown that you get the best of your day for every minute spent writing on a planner.

It is a very common complaint that hours and days feel like they are slipping through your fingers. You may feel like you're constantly playing catch-up. *You're not alone.*

Modern life is fast-paced, demanding, and chaotic. Balancing work, school, family, and personal time can seem like an insurmountable challenge. This is where time management comes into play, and it's not just for the naturally organized. It's a skill that can be honed and improved with practice.

In this chapter, we will explore five time management techniques that are not only popular but incredibly effective. These techniques can help you regain control over your schedule, reduce stress, and boost your overall productivity. The key is to find the method that resonates with you the most. Don't worry if it takes a little time to settle into a groove – like mastering any skill, patience is essential.

To make things more relatable and engaging, let me introduce you to Sarah, a college student with a fairly packed schedule. Typically, her day is divided into sleeping, school, dance practice, social engagement, homework and projects, and her fair share of extracurricular activities. Here's what her schedule generally looks like:

Day	Time	Activities
Monday	7:00 AM - 8:00 AM	Wake up and morning routine
	8:00 AM - 3:00 PM	School
	3:00 PM - 4:00 PM	Homework/Studying
	4:00 PM - 6:00 PM	Dance practice
	6:00 PM - 8:00 PM	Social time and dinner
	8:00 PM - 9:00 PM	Homework
	9:00 PM - 10:00 PM	Relaxation and unwind
	10:00 PM	Bedtime
Tuesday	7:00 AM - 8:00 AM	Wake up and morning routine
	8:00 AM - 3:00 PM	School
	3:00 PM - 4:00 PM	Homework/Studying
	4:00 PM - 6:00 PM	Dance practice
	6:00 PM - 8:00 PM	Dinner and leisure time
	8:00 PM - 9:00 PM	Homework
	9:00 PM - 10:00 PM	Relaxation and unwind
	10:00 PM	Bedtime
Wednesday	7:00 AM - 8:00 AM	Wake up and morning routine
	8:00 AM - 3:00 PM	School
	3:00 PM - 4:00 PM	Homework/Studying
	4:00 PM - 6:00 PM	Dance practice
	6:00 PM - 8:00 PM	Social time and dinner
	8:00 PM - 9:00 PM	Homework/Studying
	9:00 PM - 10:00 PM	Relaxation and unwind
	10:00 PM	Bedtime
Thursday	7:00 AM - 8:00 AM	Wake up and morning routine
	8:00 AM - 3:00 PM	School
	3:00 PM - 6:00 PM	Homework/Studying
	6:00 PM - 8:00 PM	Dinner and leisure time
	8:00 PM - 9:00 PM	Homework/Studying
	9:00 PM - 10:00 PM	Relaxation and unwind
	10:00 PM	Bedtime

Friday	7:00 AM - 8:00 AM	Wake up and morning routine
	8:00 AM - 3:00 PM	School
	3:00 PM - 4:00 PM	Homework/Studying
	4:00 PM - 6:00 PM	Dance practice
	6:00 PM - 8:00 PM	Social time and dinner
	8:00 PM - 9:00 PM	Homework/Studying
	9:00 PM - 10:00 PM	Relaxation and unwind
	10:00 PM	Bedtime
Saturday	8:00 AM - 9:00 AM	Wake up and morning routine
	9:00 AM - 12:00 PM	Leisure time
	12:00 PM - 1:00 PM	Lunch
	1:00 PM - 3:00 PM	Homework/Studying
	3:00 PM - 5:00 PM	Social engagement
	5:00 PM - 8:00 PM	Relaxation and leisure time
	8:00 PM	Bedtime
Sunday	8:00 AM - 9:00 AM	Wake up and morning routine
	9:00 AM - 12:00 PM	Leisure time
	12:00 PM - 1:00 PM	Lunch
	1:00 PM - 3:00 PM	Homework/Studying
	3:00 PM - 5:00 PM	Extracurricular activities
	5:00 PM - 8:00 PM	Relaxation and leisure time
	8:00 PM	Bedtime

While this schedule seems to be very straightforward and well-aligned, Murphy's Law suggests that something will happen that is most likely going to disrupt her schedule. She'll have to fit some new things in between her commitments and plan the entire day accordingly. Furthermore, this schedule will also have to change when exams are near.

For now, she has recently gotten some new homework and projects that she must complete within specific deadlines. Her friends are also asking her to go to the movies with them. The engagement she needs to fit in include:

- Homework assignment for Psychology due 24 hours from now,
- Homework assignment for History due 3 days from now,
- Homework assignment for Chemistry due 3 days from now,
- Small project for Art class due 4 days from now,
- Big project for Business Studies due 9 days from now,
- Dance practice sessions (2 hours each) on Wednesday & Friday,
- Movie plans with friends Weekend, 3 PM.

In the following sections, we'll dive into five popular and highly effective time management techniques to help individuals like Sarah manage their schedules more efficiently and maximize productivity.

Let's explore each technique, understand how it works, and uncover the evidence behind its effectiveness.

TIME BLOCKING:

Time blocking is a highly effective time management technique that involves scheduling specific blocks of time for various tasks and activities. This approach enables you to dedicate focused time to essential tasks, significantly boosting productivity.

Let's explore how time blocking works and the benefits it offers.

How Time Blocking Works

Sarah's schedule is an excellent example to illustrate how time blocking can be implemented effectively. Given her busy routine, she can allocate specific blocks of time to different tasks and responsibilities.

Here's how Sarah can adapt her schedule using time blocking:

- **Prioritization**: Identify top priorities, balancing academic tasks, dance practice, and relaxation.
- **To-Do List**: Create a comprehensive to-do list for personal and academic tasks.
- **Task Batching**: Group similar tasks together, allocating specific time blocks for focused studying, homework, and dance practice.
- **Day Theming**: Implement day theming for broader task categories, dedicating specific days to academic work and extracurricular activities.
- **Timeboxing**: Allocate dedicated time for future tasks, such as reserving Wednesday and Friday mornings for assignment preparation.
- **Finding the "Best" Time**: Schedule mentally demanding tasks during peak productivity hours to enhance efficiency and focus.

- **Anticipating Unforeseen Demands**: Allocate a daily block for urgent tasks, providing flexibility to address unforeseen demands without compromising the overall schedule.

To visualize these changes, here's a sample of how Sarah might modify her Monday's schedule using time blocking:

Day	Time	Activities
	7:00 AM - 8:00 AM	Wake up and morning routine
	8:00 AM - 3:00 PM	School
	3:00 PM - 4:00 PM	Homework/Studying (Time Blocking: Focused Study)
	4:00 PM - 6:00 PM	Dance practice (Time Blocking: Dance Practice)
Monday	6:00 PM - 7:00 PM	Social time
	7:00 PM - 8:00 PM	Dinner
	8:00 PM - 9:00 PM	Homework (Time Blocking: Homework)
	9:00 PM - 10:00 PM	Relaxation and unwind
	10:00 PM	Bedtime

Benefits of Time Blocking

Time blocking offers a range of benefits, including:

1. **Improved Focus**: By allocating dedicated time to specific tasks, you can concentrate better and reduce distractions, leading to more efficient work.
2. **Prioritization**: It encourages you to identify and prioritize essential tasks, ensuring that critical responsibilities receive adequate attention.

3. **Task Completion**: Tasks are completed faster with more attention to detail, as you can focus completely on the job at hand.

4. **Procrastination Reduction**: With allotted time to begin and complete tasks, time blocking helps eliminate procrastination.

5. **Efficiency**: Similar tasks are grouped together, allowing for more efficient completion and reducing the time spent switching between unrelated activities.

6. **Understanding Task Duration**: Time blocking provides insights into how long tasks take, aiding in future scheduling and commitments.

However, it's important to note that time blocking might not be suitable for everyone, especially if your role involves constant adjustments and impromptu tasks.

THE POMODORO TECHNIQUE

The Pomodoro Technique is a time management method developed in the late 1980s by a university student named Francesco Cirillo. Cirillo created this technique to help him overcome the challenges of focus and productivity. Overwhelmed by his studies, he decided to make a commitment to just 10 minutes of focused study time. To mark these intervals, he used a kitchen timer in the shape of a tomato, "pomodoro" in Italian, and thus, the Pomodoro Technique was born.

How Pomodoro Technique Works

The simplicity of this technique is one of its key strengths. To implement the Pomodoro Technique, you need a to-do list and a timer. Here's how it works:

- **Set a timer for 25 minutes**: Choose a specific task or activity you want to work on.
- **Focus on that task**: Work on the chosen task with complete concentration until the timer rings. This 25-minute interval is known as a "Pomodoro."
- **Mark your progress**: After each Pomodoro, mark off your accomplishment and take a short 5-minute break.
- **After four Pomodoros**: After completing four Pomodoros, take a longer break of 15-30 minutes to rest and recharge.

The core of the Pomodoro Technique is these 25-minute work sprints. In addition to this, there are three rules to maximize the benefits:

- **Break down complex projects**: If a task requires more than four Pomodoros to complete, break it down into smaller, actionable steps. This helps maintain clarity and progress.
- **Group small tasks**: Tasks that can be completed in less than one Pomodoro should be grouped together. For example, you can tackle multiple

simple tasks like "write rent check," "set a vet appointment," and "read Pomodoro article" in one Pomodoro.

- **Pomodoro integrity**: Once you start a Pomodoro, it should not be interrupted, especially not for checking emails, team chats, or text messages. Any new ideas, tasks, or requests should be noted and addressed later.

If an unavoidable disruption occurs, you can take your 5-minute break and start a new Pomodoro. Cirillo also suggests tracking interruptions and finding ways to avoid them in the future.

Benefits of The Pomodoro Technique

The Pomodoro Technique has proven to be effective for several reasons:

1. **Making it easy to get started**: Procrastination often stems from the fear of starting a daunting task. The Pomodoro Technique combats this by breaking big tasks into small, manageable 25-minute intervals. Instead of facing the entire project, you only need to focus on the next Pomodoro.

2. **Combating distractions**: Distractions can be a significant productivity killer. The Pomodoro Technique helps you stay on track by dedicating

each Pomodoro to a single task and providing breaks for regaining focus.

3. **Becoming more aware of your time**: This method helps you gain a better understanding of how long tasks take, which can lead to more realistic time estimates for future projects. It changes your perception of time, making it a measure of productivity rather than a source of anxiety.

4. **Gamifying your productivity**: Each Pomodoro offers a chance to improve upon the last. The focus is on consistency rather than perfection, and you can challenge yourself to complete more Pomodoros each day.

For Sarah's schedule, for example, she will implement the Pomodoro Technique on her typical Tuesdays as follows:

Day	Time	Activities	Pomodoros Implemented
	7:00 AM - 8:00 AM	Wake-up/morning routine	N/A
	8:00 AM - 3:00 PM	School	N/A
	3:00 PM - 4:00 PM	Homework/Studying	1
	4:00 PM - 6:00 PM	Dance practice	2
Tuesday	6:00 PM - 8:00 PM	Dinner and leisure time	N/A
	8:00 PM - 9:00 PM	Homework	1
	9:00 PM - 10:00 PM	Relaxation and unwind	1
	10:00 PM	Bedtime	N/A

EAT THE FROG METHOD

The "Eat the Frog" method is a time management technique that encourages you to tackle your most challenging or important task at the beginning of the day, which is often symbolically referred to as "eating the frog." The idea is that once you've completed the most challenging task, everything else will feel more manageable.

How the Eat the Frog Method Works

The core principle of the Eat the Frog method is to identify the most important task or project for the day and start working on it as soon as possible. Here's how you can implement this technique:

1. **Identify your "frog:"** Your "frog" is the most critical, challenging, or important task you need to accomplish. It's something that might be weighing on your mind or demanding significant mental effort.
2. **Start your day with the frog:** As soon as you begin your workday, dive into your frog task. Don't check your email or social media or get distracted with minor tasks. This focused effort on the most important task sets a productive tone for the day.
3. **Focus on completion:** Work on your frog task until it's completed or until you've made

substantial progress. Avoid multitasking and give it your full attention.

4. **Celebrate your accomplishment:** Once you've finished your frog task, take a moment to acknowledge your achievement. You've already tackled the most challenging part of your day.

5. **Proceed with other tasks:** After completing your frog task, you can move on to other less demanding tasks with a sense of accomplishment.

Benefits of the Eat the Frog Method

The Eat the Frog method offers several advantages:

1. **Enhanced productivity:** Starting your day with the most challenging task ensures that you make significant progress early, boosting overall productivity.

2. **Reduced procrastination:** By addressing the most challenging task first, you avoid the temptation to procrastinate or delay it.

3. **Reduced stress:** Accomplishing your most critical task early in the day can reduce stress and anxiety, making the rest of the day feel more manageable.

4. **Improved focus:** Prioritizing your frog task means you can give it your undivided attention and complete it more efficiently.

Now, let's see how Sarah will implement the Eat the Frog method on a typical Wednesday:

Time	Activities	Implementation of Eat the Frog Method
7:00 AM - 8:00 AM	Wake up and morning routine	N/A
8:00 AM - 3:00 PM	School	N/A
3:00 PM - 4:00 PM	Homework/Studying	**Eat the Frog: Homework**
4:00 PM - 6:00 PM	Dance practice	N/A
6:00 PM - 7:00 PM	Social time	N/A
7:00 PM - 8:00 PM	Dinner	N/A
8:00 PM - 9:00 PM	Homework/Studying	N/A
9:00 PM - 10:00 PM	Relaxation and unwind	N/A
10:00 PM	Bedtime	N/A

Sarah is implementing the Eat the Frog method on Wednesday for her homework. She has a dedicated study session from 3:00 PM to 4:00 PM, immediately after school.

She will focus on her most challenging or important homework assignment during this time. By tackling this assignment first, she ensures that she starts her work on a productive note, avoids procrastination, and reduces stress.

The "Eat the Frog: Homework" label in the table indicates where she has applied this method. Starting her homework as soon as she's done with school allows her to address her most critical tasks early in the day, leading to enhanced productivity and a more manageable day overall.

MAKER/MANAGER SCHEDULE

The Maker/Manager Schedule is a productivity technique that recognizes two types of work schedules: maker and manager schedules. Makers are individuals who need long, uninterrupted blocks of time to focus on creative and complex tasks, such as writing, coding, or designing. Conversely, managers work in shorter, more fragmented time blocks, often filled with meetings, emails, and decision-making.

Benefits of the Maker/Manager Schedule

1. **Enhanced Focus:** This method allows makers to allocate undistracted blocks of time for creative work, leading to improved focus and productivity.
2. **Reduced Context Switching:** By separating maker and manager tasks, individuals can minimize the disruptions caused by constant context switching, leading to more efficient work.
3. **Improved Creativity:** Makers can harness their peak creative energy during dedicated periods, resulting in higher-quality outputs.

4. **Efficient Decision-Making:** Managers can allocate specific time blocks for making decisions and handling administrative tasks, ensuring these are done effectively.

Implementation on a Typical Thursday

Here's a table illustrating how Sarah can implement the Maker/Manager Schedule technique in her typical Thursday schedule:

Time	Activities	Implementation of Maker/Manager Schedule
7:00 AM - 8:00 AM	Wake up and morning routine	N/A
8:00 AM - 3:00 PM	School	Manager (managerial tasks at school)
3:00 PM - 5:00 PM	Homework/Studying	Maker (focused study)
5:00 PM - 6:00 PM	Dinner and leisure time	Manager (relaxation, no work tasks)
6:00 PM - 8:00 PM	Homework/Studying	Maker (focused study)
8:00 PM - 9:00 PM	Homework/Studying	Manager (shorter tasks, review)
9:00 PM - 10:00 PM	Relaxation and unwind	Manager (unwinding, planning for tomorrow)
10:00 PM	Bedtime	N/A

The idea is that:

- **Manager Tasks:** Sarah treats her time at school (8:00 AM - 3:00 PM) as manager time since she deals with classes, teachers, and managerial tasks.

This is where she might have meetings, take notes, and engage in school-related managerial activities.

- **Maker Tasks:** From 3:00 PM to 5:00 PM and then again from 6:00 PM to 8:00 PM, Sarah allocates maker time for focused studying and tackling homework assignments. During these time blocks, she can deeply concentrate on her academic work without interruptions.

- **Balancing Manager Tasks:** Sarah dedicates 8:00 PM to 9:00 PM as manager time for shorter tasks related to homework, such as reviewing her work, making to-do lists, and planning for the next day.

- **Relaxation and Unwind:** The evening hours (9:00 PM - 10:00 PM) are allocated to manager tasks, which include relaxing, unwinding, and planning for the next day, ensuring she winds down effectively.

This approach helps Sarah make the most of her maker hours for in-depth study and academic work and efficiently manages her manager hours to maintain a balanced schedule.

PARKINSON'S LAW

Parkinson's Law is a time management and productivity principle suggesting that work expands to fill the time available for completion. In other words, if you have a task to complete and allocate more time to it than necessary, you're likely to take that extra time, even if it could be done more quickly. Conversely, setting shorter, more focused deadlines makes you more likely to complete the task within that time frame.

Benefits of Parkinson's Law

1. **Enhanced Focus:** It encourages individuals to concentrate on the most critical aspects of a task and avoid unnecessary delays.
2. **Improved Productivity:** By setting shorter deadlines, people can become more productive and complete tasks more efficiently.
3. **Reduced Procrastination:** Knowing there's a limited time for a task can help individuals overcome procrastination and focus on the job at hand.
4. **Better Time Management:** Parkinson's Law promotes better time management by preventing the wastage of excess time on a task.

Implementation on a Typical Friday

Here's a table illustrating how Sarah can implement Parkinson's Law in her typical Friday schedule:

Time	Activities	Implementation of Parkinson's Law
7:00 AM - 8:00 AM	Wake up and morning routine	N/A
8:00 AM - 3:00 PM	School	N/A
3:00 PM - 4:00 PM	Homework/Studying	Set a focused, shorter deadline for completing a specific part of her homework.
4:00 PM - 6:00 PM	Dance practice	Apply Parkinson's Law by setting a focused time frame for practicing her dance moves.
6:00 PM - 8:00 PM	Social time and dinner	Enjoy social time without overextending the duration of dinner.
8:00 PM - 9:00 PM	Homework/Studying	Use Parkinson's Law by allocating a shorter time frame to complete another part of her homework.
9:00 PM - 10:00 PM	Relaxation and unwind	Wind down within a specific time frame.
10:00 PM	Bedtime	N/A

The idea is to implement the law as follows:

- **Homework/Studying:** Sarah can set specific, shorter deadlines for her homework assignments and make an effort to complete each part within the given time frame. For example, she might decide to finish a particular reading or a section of an assignment within 45 minutes, thus applying Parkinson's Law to keep her study sessions efficient.
- **Dance Practice:** When practicing her dance moves from 4:00 PM to 6:00 PM, she can set a

focused time frame for each dance routine. By doing so, she ensures that her practice remains productive and doesn't linger on a single routine for too long.

- **Dinner:** During her social time and dinner (6:00 PM - 8:00 PM), Sarah can enjoy dinner without letting it extend beyond a reasonable time frame.
- **Relaxation and Unwind:** To ensure she gets adequate rest, Sarah can allocate a specific time frame for relaxation and unwinding, thus preventing unnecessary delays in her evening wind-down routine.

By applying Parkinson's Law, Sarah can avoid time wastage and maintain a more efficient schedule on her typical Friday.

ACCOMPLISHING SPECIFIC TASKS WITH THESE TECHNIQUES

Sarah can use each time management technique separately to accomplish her objectives. This is an example of how she can do that:

1. **Task**: Homework assignment due in 24 hours

    a. **Time Management Technique**: Eat the Frog Method
    b. **Implementation**: Sarah will allocate a dedicated

block of time to complete the homework assignment. To eat the frog, she will start working on it as soon as possible, preferably early in the day when her focus is high. For instance, Sarah will allocate 3:00 PM to 4:00 PM on Monday to focus on the assignment due in 24 hours.

2. **Task**: 2 homework assignments for two different classes due in 3 days

   a. **Time Management Technique**: Time Blocking

   b. **Implementation**: Sarah will use time blocking to allocate specific time blocks for each homework assignment. For example, on Tuesday, she can allocate the afternoon to focus on one assignment (3:00 PM - 4:00 PM) and later allocate time on Wednesday for the second assignment (e.g., 5:00 PM - 6:00 PM).

3. **Task**: Small project due in 4 days

   a. **Time Management Technique**: Parkinson's Law

   b. **Implementation**: Sarah can apply Parkinson's Law to work efficiently on her small project. By setting shorter deadlines and focusing her efforts, she can work on the project during a specific time block. For instance, she might allocate 3:00 PM to 4:30 PM on Thursday to complete the small project.

4. Task: Big project due in 9 days

    a. Time Management Technique: Maker/Manager Schedule

    b. Implementation: Sarah can use the Maker/Manager Schedule to effectively manage her time for the big project. During maker hours, she can allocate larger blocks of uninterrupted time for research and initial planning. During manager hours, she can schedule time for smaller tasks related to the project, such as reviewing her progress or making a to-do list. This can be done on Thursday, allocating 3:00 PM to 5:00 PM as maker hours and 8:00 PM to 9:00 PM as manager hours.

5. Task: Dance practice on Wednesday and Friday, for 2 hours each session

    a. Time Management Technique: Time Blocking

    b. Implementation: Sarah can use time blocking to allocate focused time for dance practice. She can set aside 4:00 PM to 6:00 PM on Wednesday and Friday for her dance practice sessions.

6. Task: Plans to see a movie with friends on the weekend at 3 PM

    a. Time Management Technique: Pomodoro Technique

    b. Implementation: Sarah can use the Pomodoro Technique on the weekend morning to ensure she doesn't lose track of time and has a productive day before going out. She can allocate Pomodoros for various tasks, ensuring she stays on track and has time for relaxation before the movie. For instance, she can use the Pomodoro Technique on Saturday morning, starting from her wake-up time, to plan her day effectively.

This combination of time management techniques will help Sarah efficiently manage her schedule and meet her various commitments and deadlines.

SAMPLE TIME BLOCKING TEMPLATE

If you're ready to start implementing one of these techniques, the easiest one to start off with is the time-blocking technique. Here is a template that you can use for creating time blocks throughout the day.

Time	Activity	Variance
8:00 AM	Morning Routine	
8:30 AM		
9:00 AM		
10:30 AM		
10:45 AM		
12:00 PM		
1:00 PM		
2:00 PM		
3:30 PM		
3:45 PM		
5:00 PM		
6:00 PM		
6:30 PM		
7:30 PM		
8:00 PM		
8:30 PM		
9:00 PM		
9:30 PM		
10:00 PM		
10:30 PM		
11:00 PM		
11:30 PM		
12:00 PM		

Remember, you don't have to allocate just one block for a specific task. You can also allot consecutive tasks, such as studying, to two or more blocks before you take a break.

In this chapter, we've explored five powerful time management techniques to help you take control of your schedule, reduce stress, and boost your productivity. Each method offers unique benefits, and it's important to find the one that resonates with you the most.

Remember, it's perfectly normal to experiment with these techniques and discover what works best for you. Like mastering any skill, patience is key, and trial and error is part of the journey to efficient time management.

We have reached the end of part one of this book, which primarily focuses on time management concepts and solutions. In part two, we'll look into the challenges and obstacles students commonly face when managing their time effectively.

MAKE YOUR BED

"And, if by chance you have a miserable day, you will come home to a bed that is made — that you made — and a made bed gives you encouragement that tomorrow will be better."

— ADMIRAL WILLIAM H. MCRAVEN

We've come a long way on our journey together now, and I'd like to remind you of the story I told you about my father in the introduction. He told me that making my bed was not just making my bed, but making my day ... and you know what? I still find that to be true now.

I don't know where my father got that piece of wisdom from, but I know where I've come across it since, and I want to share it with you so you can see how much of an impact this mindset has.

There's a rousing speech by Admiral William H. McRaven —look it up online. I promise you it's worth it. He recounts 10 lessons he learned from basic Navy SEAL training that he believes are powerful things to apply to every area of life. One of these lessons was to make your bed—to the exact specifications required in the Navy.

This task, he believes, was never really about making the bed. It was about starting the day with a sense of pride, encouraging you to do the next task ... and the next one ... and the next. It was a way to motivate yourself to do every task, and it was a way to demonstrate that the little things matter. The little things are the foundation for the big things.

It is my hope that this book is part of that foundation, giving you everything you need to move forward from success to success ... and I'd like to ask you to take a few minutes to help me reach more young people with this message.

By leaving a review of this book on Amazon, you'll help other teenagers find these essential time management and life skills—skills I know you're now truly understanding the importance of.

A huge part of life is the kindness we extend to others, and simply by leaving this review, you're practicing this skill powerfully. Sharing information is a wonderful way to help others, and by leaving your feedback online, you'll be doing just that.

Thank you so much for your support. Make your bed and help others: I don't know if there are two more important pieces of advice I could give you.

5

TIME VS. TECHNOLOGY

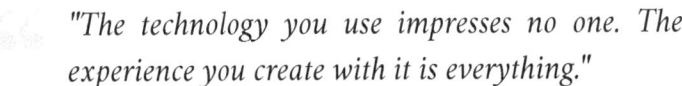

"The technology you use impresses no one. The experience you create with it is everything."

— SEAN GERETY

Our daily lives are increasingly entwined with technology. The pervasive use of the internet and digital devices has become integral to modern living, shaping how we work, socialize, and navigate the world. According to recent statistics, global internet users spent an average of six hours and forty minutes online every day during the first quarter of 2023, reflecting a 0.8% increase compared to the previous quarter.

This amount of time spent in the digital world highlights technology's profound impact on our daily routines. As we navigate this landscape, evaluating not just the quantity but the quality of our technological interactions becomes crucial. The convenience and efficiency offered by digital tools can significantly enhance productivity. But a mindful approach to technology usage is essential to prevent it from becoming a double-edged sword.

In this chapter, we will look into the relationship between time and technology, exploring how digital advancements can both empower and impede our productivity. We will introduce concepts such as mindful technology use and the importance of periodic digital detoxes in maintaining a healthy balance between our online and offline lives.

WHEN TECHNOLOGY HINDERS

Ironically, in the pursuit of efficiency, technology can become a hindrance, subtly eroding productivity in various aspects of our lives. This is particularly the case for students and teenagers. Several elements of technology can act as impediments rather than enablers.

1. **Digital Distractions**: Devices designed to enhance learning can turn into distraction hubs. Social media, messaging, and notifications disrupt focus, challenging students in studies or creative endeavors.
2. **Information Overload**: The internet's vast information pool overwhelms students. Navigating through data becomes a skill, but the

constant influx leads to cognitive overload, hindering deep learning.

3. **Multitasking Myth**: The digital age touts multitasking as a productivity boon, but research reveals reduced efficiency and compromised learning. Technology facilitates multitasking but sacrifices focused in-depth engagement.

4. **Sedentary Lifestyle**: Immersive technology usage contributes to a sedentary lifestyle. Prolonged screen time leads to fatigue, eye strain, and diminished overall well-being, impacting physical health and cognitive function.

5. **Loss of Creativity**: Despite offering creative tools, technology reliance stifles organic, imaginative thinking. Exposure to pre-programmed templates and algorithms hampers the development of unique ideas and solutions.

6. **Dependence on Productivity Apps**: Productivity apps aim to streamline tasks but can diminish self-management skills with excessive use. Students may rely on reminders, reducing their ability to structure and organize their work independently.

Let's consider three examples, highlighting a unique way in which technology can interfere with one's productivity.

The Google Dependency Dilemma:

Emma, a diligent student, found herself in the clutches of a digital conundrum. She relied heavily on Google for immediate answers and discovered that her once-prized research skills had withered away.

Writing research papers became a struggle as she bypassed the traditional process of in-depth exploration, proper sourcing, and citations. The ease of Google searches led her into a web of instant gratification, making it challenging to produce well-researched and substantiated academic work.

The allure of immediate answers became a stumbling block on her path to scholarly excellence.

The TikTok Time Warp:

James, a conscientious student, faced a different digital dilemma during his allotted study breaks. Initially intending to take a brief respite, he found himself entrapped in the infinite scroll of TikTok and other social media platforms.

Constant recommendations and the captivating allure of endless content led him to lose track of time. What began as a brief 10-minute break morphed into an extended session of mindless scrolling, leaving James disoriented and squandering valuable study time.

The very platforms designed for entertainment and relaxation became unassuming thieves of his precious hours.

The App Overload Odyssey:

Sarah, an ambitious student with a penchant for productivity, began her journey laden with productivity apps. Seeking to optimize every aspect of her academic and personal life, she downloaded numerous applications.

However, the abundance of tools designed to enhance efficiency paradoxically led to a wasteful cycle of app-hopping. Constantly switching from one app to another became a time-consuming endeavor, leaving Sarah in a state of perpetual transition rather than focused action.

Her pursuit of productivity became ensnared in the complexity of managing multiple applications, inadvertently impeding the very efficiency she sought.

These stories showcase ways technology, if not approached mindfully, can impede our productivity, transforming tools into impediments and distractions.

WHEN TECHNOLOGY HELPS

While the pitfalls of technology are apparent, it's crucial to acknowledge that, when used judiciously, technology can be a potent ally in enhancing time management skills and overall productivity.

Let's dive into how students can harness the positive aspects of technology to accomplish their goals and elevate their efficiency.

Strategic Goal Setting:

Technology provides a myriad of tools to facilitate goal setting. From dedicated goal-setting apps to calendar reminders, students can leverage digital platforms to establish and track their objectives. These tools act as digital compasses, guiding users toward their academic, personal, and professional milestones.

Entrapped in the Google Dependency Dilemma, Emma could employ goal-setting apps to regain control over her research process.

Task Management Apps:

Productivity apps can be a game-changer when it comes to managing tasks. Unlike the limitations of paper planners, digital task management apps offer dynamic features such as:

- Real-time updates,
- Synchronization across devices and
- Interactive interfaces.

For instance, James could benefit from task management apps during his study breaks. By allocating specific time blocks for social media and integrating reminders, he could avoid the infinite scroll, ensuring that breaks remain refreshing without spiraling into unproductive procrastination.

Collaborative Platforms:

When it comes to group projects and collaborative assignments, technology emerges as a facilitator. Platforms like Google Workspace and Microsoft Teams foster seamless collaboration, allowing students to work collectively on documents, presentations, and projects.

For example, Sarah, entangled in the App Overload Odyssey, could streamline her academic pursuits using collaborative platforms. Instead of juggling multiple apps, she could consolidate tasks on platforms like Microsoft Teams.

Automation for Efficiency:

Automation tools can streamline repetitive tasks, saving time and reducing the risk of oversight. Features like automated reminders, calendar events, and email filters contribute to efficient time management.

While striving for efficient research, Emma could automate reminders for each stage of her paper-writing process. Automation would assist her in maintaining a structured approach, preventing the quicksand of unproductive shortcuts facilitated by the instant-gratification nature of Google searches.

Digital Learning Resources:

Technology has revolutionized the accessibility of educational resources. E-books, online courses, and digital libraries provide students with instant access to a wealth of knowledge. This accessibility enhances the learning experience, allowing students to dive into diverse subjects and stay abreast of the latest developments in their field.

For instance, James, between his TikTok breaks, could incorporate digital learning resources to make those breaks not only entertaining but also educational.

Data Analysis & Insights:

Analytical tools integrated into productivity apps offer valuable insights into usage patterns. By assessing how time is allocated across various tasks, students can identify areas for improvement and optimize their study routines.

Data-driven insights empower students to make informed decisions about their time management strategies. Sarah, navigating the complexities of multiple productivity apps, could leverage data analysis tools to gain insights into her usage patterns.

Flexibility and Adaptability:

Digital tools offer unparalleled flexibility. Unlike traditional methods, technology allows for swift adjustments to schedules and plans. Last-minute changes can be seamlessly accommodated, and students can adapt their study routines based on evolving priorities and unexpected challenges.

Each of the three stories could benefit from the flexibility offered by technology. Whether adapting research strategies, optimizing break times, or refining app usage, technology's adaptability aligns with the evolving needs and challenges students like Emma, James, and Sarah face in their academic journeys.

Why Embrace Productivity Apps?

While the effectiveness of a paper planner is undeniable, productivity apps present a different set of advantages. The digital landscape offers dynamic features that cater to the evolving needs of a tech-savvy generation. Real-time updates, cloud synchronization, and interactive interfaces provide a level of flexibility and convenience that traditional planners may lack. Embracing productivity apps is not about discarding time-tested methods but rather integrating the strengths of digital tools to enhance overall productivity and adaptability in the face of a rapidly changing academic landscape.

By intentionally navigating the digital landscape and leveraging technology wisely, students can transform it from a potential hindrance into a powerful asset in their academic journey.

IMPLEMENTING A DIGITAL DETOX: RECLAIMING BALANCE

In the digital age, a term has emerged to counteract the overwhelming influence of technology on our lives: *Digital Detox*.

It's a conscious and temporary break from the digital world, allowing individuals, especially teenagers, to recalibrate and regain control over their offline lives. But why is it important, and how can someone like James, deeply immersed in the world of TikTok, benefit from it?

Understanding Digital Detox:

A digital detox involves intentionally unplugging from electronic devices, including smartphones, computers, and social media platforms. Its importance, particularly for teenagers, lies in mitigating the adverse effects of excessive screen time. These may include:

- Sleep disturbances,
- Heightened stress levels,
- Inability to focus, and
- Diminished social abilities.

It promotes improved mental well-being, fosters healthier sleep patterns, and encourages face-to-face interactions, which are crucial for adolescent development.

How to Digitally Detox

Implementing a digital detox requires a strategic approach. Teens can start by setting clear goals for their detox period, whether it's a day, a weekend, or longer. Creating a physical space away from screens, engaging in outdoor activities, and spending quality time with family and friends are effective ways to reset.

For James, the TikTok enthusiast, a digital detox might initially seem daunting. However, he can ease into it by gradually reducing his screen time. James could designate specific hours in the evening as "*Tech-Free Time*," creating a buffer before bedtime.

During this period, he can replace TikTok scrolling with activities like reading, drawing, gardening, or pursuing another hobby.

To reinforce this change, James might consider temporarily uninstalling TikTok from his phone or using app blockers to limit access during detox hours. This intentional break allows him to rediscover the joy of offline activities, fostering a healthier balance between screen time and other aspects of life.

I recall when my fascination with the Nintendo Entertainment System (NES) consumed much of my attention. It wasn't until I decided to undergo a digital detox, limiting my gaming time and focusing on other pursuits, that I realized its transformative impact.

Just as my NES detox facilitated personal growth, today's teenagers, including James, can harness the benefits of a digital detox. It's not about abandoning technology but regaining control, nurturing a healthier relationship with digital devices, and creating space for personal development. In the process, they may discover a more balanced and fulfilling approach to life beyond the screen.

TECHNOLOGY: MINDFUL USAGE

Today, the world is dominated by digital devices. You'll find the latest iPhone or a gaming laptop with children much younger than yourself. As a result, fostering mindful technology use is essential, especially for students navigating the dynamic landscape of the online world.

With technology addiction looming as a genuine concern, adopting mindful habits early on is a proactive step toward a balanced and productive relationship with digital tools.

Mindful technology use involves intentional and aware interaction with digital devices. By implementing mindful habits, students can prevent technology from becoming a source of distraction, stress, or addiction.

Educating oneself about healthy technology practices and incorporating simple strategies into daily routines can significantly contribute to overall well-being.

STRATEGIES FOR MINDFUL TECHNOLOGY USE:

1. Turn Off Notifications:

To declutter the digital bombardment, turn off non-essential notifications. By curating your alerts, you can tailor your focus to the tasks at hand without being incessantly pulled into the whirlwind of the digital world.

This intentional approach promotes a serene environment for concentration and reduces the urge to respond reactively to every ping. for example, turning off non-essential notifications can address Emma's struggle with distractions.

By curating her alerts, she can regain control over her focus during research and writing, preventing the incessant pings from Google searches that disrupt her scholarly pursuits. This intentional approach promotes a serene environment for concentration, countering the distraction hub that technology had become for Emma.

2. Device-Free Meal Times:

Transform meal times into sanctuaries of connection by designating them as device-free zones. Immerse yourself in the sensory experience of enjoying your meals without the distraction of screens.

Not only does this practice foster mindful eating, but it also creates opportunities for meaningful connections during shared family or social gatherings, strengthening the bonds that extend beyond the digital interface.

For the stories above, designating meal times as device-free can align with James' struggle against the infinite scroll. By establishing sacred moments without screens, he can break free from the captivating allure of social media platforms during his breaks.

This practice will not only enhance mindful eating but also prevent James from losing track of time in the digital vortex, fostering more intentional and meaningful breaks.

3. Grayscale Screens:

Transition your devices into grayscale mode, especially during the evening hours. The absence of vibrant colors in this mode is not only aesthetically calming but also serves a functional purpose.

By reducing the visual allure of the screen, grayscale mode creates an environment that is less tempting and more conducive to winding down before bedtime. This subtle shift supports a more peaceful transition into a restful night's sleep.

For example, setting devices to grayscale mode may help Sarah overcome her challenge with excessive productivity apps. The grayscale setting, with its subdued visual appeal, diminishes the allure of the screen.

This subtle shift aligns with Sarah's need to streamline her digital experience, making it less tempting and conducive to effective time management. It's a strategy to break free from the complex cycle of app-hopping that hindered Sarah's pursuit of productivity.

4. Screen-Free Wind Down:

Embrace a screen-free wind-down ritual by abstaining from smartphone or screen-based device usage at least 60 minutes before bedtime. The blue light emitted by screens can interfere with the natural production of melatonin, the sleep-inducing hormone.

By disconnecting from screens, you create a buffer zone that allows your mind to unwind, improving the quality of your sleep and contributing to overall well-being.

James can make use of this strategy effectively. Avoiding screens at least 60 minutes before bedtime can help James' struggle with time management during study breaks. This practice will counter the tendency to lose track of time in the evening, offering a better balance between digital engagement and restful sleep.

5. Offline Support System:

Cultivate a robust offline support system to counterbalance the digital domain. Engage in sports, engage with hobbies, spend quality time with friends, or pursue other interests that exist beyond the confines of the digital sphere.

By diversifying your activities, you create a more holistic and fulfilling lifestyle that extends beyond the virtual world, promoting a healthy balance between the online and offline aspects of your life.

Consider Sarah's App Overload, for instance. Cultivating an offline support system means engaging in sports, hobbies, and socializing outside the digital world. This will reinforce the importance of a balanced life for her.

6. Connect with Nature:

Reconnect with the natural world by spending intentional time outdoors. Whether it's a leisurely walk in the park, lying on the grass and gazing at the sky, or simply immersing yourself in the soothing sounds of nature, these activities offer a refreshing break from the screen-centric hustle.

Nature provides a rejuvenating backdrop that invigorates your senses and restores a sense of balance in your daily routine. Spending time outdoors and connecting with nature speaks to Emma's overreliance on immediate answers from Google. Nature can encourage Emma to step back from constant searches and immerse herself in a more organic environment.

7. Mindfulness Techniques:

Embrace mindfulness techniques as powerful tools for enhancing focus and curbing the incessant urge for constant digital stimulation. Incorporate activities such as deep breathing exercises, meditation sessions, or mindful awareness practices into your daily routine.

These simple yet profound techniques empower you to navigate the digital landscape intentionally, promoting mental clarity and fostering a mindful approach to technology use. The idea is to break free of the attachment you have with technology. This may also be *why smartphones go to therapy - they have too many attachment issues!*

RECOMMENDED PRODUCTIVITY & ORGANIZATION APPS

Here's a checklist of highly-rated and recommended scheduling and organization apps that you can use to manage your productivity:

1. Todoist:

    a. A powerful task management app with intuitive features.
    b. Organize tasks, set deadlines, and prioritize assignments efficiently.

2. Forest:

    a. Encourages focused work sessions with a unique gamified approach.
    b. Plant a virtual tree during work sessions to build a "forest" and discourage phone use.

3. Evernote:

    a. Capture and organize notes, ideas, and resources in one place.
    b. Syncs across devices, making it easy to access information anytime, anywhere.

4. Google Calendar:

    a. A versatile scheduling app for planning classes, study sessions, and extracurricular activities.
    b. Set reminders and share calendars with peers for collaborative planning.

5. Trello:

    a. Visual project management tool using boards, lists, and cards.
    b. Ideal for organizing study groups, collaborative projects, and personal to-dos.

6. Forest:

    a. Promotes focus and time management by using the Pomodoro Technique.
    b. Set work intervals (focus sessions) and breaks to enhance productivity.

7. RescueTime:

    a. Tracks screen time and app usage to provide insights into digital habits.
    b. Helps students understand and optimize their time on devices.

8. Notion:

a. An all-in-one workspace for notes, tasks, wikis, and collaborative projects.
b. Customizable templates for creating personalized study plans and project boards.

9. Quizlet:

a. An excellent app for creating and studying flashcards.
b. Boosts memory retention through interactive quizzes and games.

10. Forest:

a. Encourages focused work sessions with a unique gamified approach.
b. Plant a virtual tree during work sessions to build a "forest" and discourage phone use.

11. Focus@Will:

a. Provides curated music channels designed to enhance focus and concentration.
b. Uses neuroscience-backed music to create an optimal environment for studying.

12. Microsoft OneNote:

   a. A versatile note-taking app with multimedia integration.
   b. Ideal for organizing lecture notes, research, and collaborative projects.

13. HabitBull:

   a. Helps build positive habits by tracking daily activities.
   b. Set goals, track progress, and stay motivated to establish effective study routines.

14. Dropbox:

   a. Cloud storage for seamless collaboration and document access.
   b. Share and sync files across devices, ensuring accessibility from anywhere.

15. Wunderlist (now part of Microsoft To Do):

   a. Simplifies task management with easy-to-use lists and reminders.
   b. Collaborate with peers on shared tasks and stay organized.

Remember, if you aren't comfortable using these technologies, as the previous chapter states, there's nothing better than having a pen-and-paper-based planner on hand!

Utilizing These Apps Effectively:

Explore the features and functionalities of each app to understand how it aligns with your study needs.

- Experiment with different apps to find the combination that complements your organizational style.
- Regularly update and synchronize your apps to ensure seamless integration and optimal performance.
- Consider combining apps for different purposes, such as using task management apps alongside note-taking apps for comprehensive organization.

The effectiveness of these apps lies in how well they integrate into your study routine. Tailor your choices based on your preferences, study habits, and overall workflow.

As we traverse the digital landscape, we find ourselves at a crossroads where technology can either amplify our productivity or become a stumbling block in our academic journey. The tales of Emma, James, and Sarah signify the dance between efficiency and distraction in the technological world.

On the one hand, carefully chosen apps, mindful tech use, and strategic planning can propel us toward enhanced focus, time management, and goal attainment. On the other, the siren call of notifications, infinite scrolls, and an overload of productivity tools can derail our efforts and steer us into uncharted waters.

Being vigilant about our online habits is akin to mastering the helm of a ship navigating the seas of information. Always be mindful of the time spent online, for what seems like a brief exploration can easily become a prolonged expedition, veering into procrastination.

6

PRODUCTIVITY VS PROCRASTINATION

"This is why we say that procrastination is essentially irrational. It doesn't make sense to do something you know is going to have negative consequences."

— DR. FUSCHIA SIROIS, PROFESSOR OF PSYCHOLOGY AT THE UNIVERSITY OF SHEFFIELD

Have you ever found yourself putting off a task until the last moment, despite knowing it will only lead to stress and subpar results? Welcome to the world of procrastination, a seemingly irrational behavior that affects many of us. Dr. Fuschia Sirois's words echo a sentiment we've all felt but might not completely understand. Why do we procrastinate when logic dictates otherwise?

In this chapter, we embark on a journey to unravel the mysteries of procrastination, particularly its prevalence among teens and young adults today. We'll delve into the psychological underpinnings, explore the societal factors contributing to this phenomenon, and, most importantly, equip you with strategies to conquer procrastination and boost your productivity.

UNDERSTANDING PROCRASTINATION: NAVIGATING THE IRRATIONAL DELAY

Procrastination, the art of delaying tasks despite knowing it leads to negative consequences, is a familiar dance for many. As we focus on the criticalities of this phenomenon, let's tackle key questions that demystify the why and how behind procrastination.

What is Procrastination?

Procrastination, at its core, is the voluntary delay of an intended action despite knowing that this delay may result in undesirable outcomes. It's choosing the allure of immediate pleasure or comfort over the long-term benefits of completing a task promptly.

To illustrate, imagine Micah, a college student with an assignment due in two weeks. She's aware that starting early and working consistently would yield a well-researched and polished paper.

However, the immediate pleasure of spending those two weeks engaging in leisure activities or binge-watching shows seems far more tempting. The consequence? Stress, last-minute panic, and a potentially subpar submission.

Why Do We Procrastinate?

The roots of procrastination focus on the complexities of human psychology. Fear of failure, a desire for perfection, or simply the preference for immediate gratification are all contributors. Our brains are wired to seek instant rewards, making it challenging to resist the allure of procrastination.

Time Inconsistency: The Present Self vs. Future Self Dilemma

One compelling concept that sheds light on procrastination is "time inconsistency." As explained by behavioral economists, our Present Self and Future Self often have conflicting interests. The Present Self seeks immediate pleasure and gratification, while the Future Self desires long-term benefits and accomplishments.

Think of it as the classic struggle between eating a tempting dessert now (Present Self's preference) versus maintaining a healthy diet for long-term well-being (Future Self's goal). The Present Self often wins in the moment, leading to procrastination.

ACTIVE PROCRASTINATION VS. PASSIVE PROCRASTINATION

Not all procrastination is created equal. Understanding the nuances between active and passive procrastination adds depth to our exploration.

Active Procrastination: A Surprising Twist

Contrary to the common belief that all procrastination is detrimental, active procrastination involves strategically delaying tasks to enhance performance. Individuals practicing active procrastination thrive under the pressure of a looming deadline, using it as a motivator rather than succumbing to stress.

Imagine a student who purposely delays starting a project until the last minute, harnessing the heightened pressure to fuel productivity. Active procrastinators navigate the fine line between delay and efficiency, turning procrastination into a tool for success.

Passive Procrastination: The Traditional Culprit

On the flip side, passive procrastination aligns more closely with the conventional understanding of procrastination. It involves delaying tasks without a strategic purpose, often leading to stress, compromised quality, and missed deadlines. The passive procrastinator succumbs to the gravitational pull of immediate pleasures without a calculated approach.

MYTH-BUSTING PROCRASTINATION: DEBUNKING COMMON MISCONCEPTIONS

Myth #1: People Who Procrastinate Have No Self-Control

Contrary to the myth, procrastination is not a straightforward issue of lacking self-control. Behavioral psychologists emphasize that procrastinating individuals might exhibit self-control in various aspects of their lives. The challenge lies in overcoming the specific psychological barriers triggering procrastination.

As someone dedicated to maintaining a healthy lifestyle, my routine consisted of regular workouts and mindful eating. However, there was one aspect I consistently procrastinated on – incorporating strength training into my fitness regimen. The weights section of the gym seemed to be shrouded in an invisible barrier that I hesitated to breach.

Contrary to the myth that procrastination equates to a lack of self-control, my discipline in maintaining a consistent workout routine contradicted this notion. It wasn't a matter of lacking willpower but a unique psychological challenge tied to the fear of the unknown and the discomfort of stepping out of my comfort zone.

Acknowledging this internal struggle was my first step toward bringing to light the complexity of procrastination. It wasn't a broad-stroke issue of self-control but a nuanced battle against the specific fears and uncertainties that held me back from embracing a new aspect of my fitness journey.

This personal journey illuminated the truth – procrastination often conceals itself in the shadows of our individual challenges, and overcoming it requires a tailored approach that addresses the unique psychological barriers each of us faces.

With this realization, I ventured into the realm of self-discovery. I developed strategies that not only conquered my gym-related procrastination but also enriched my understanding of the delicate interplay between self-control and the complex psychology behind procrastination.

Myth #2: People Who Procrastinate Are Lazy

Procrastination, often unfairly synonymous with laziness, hides a more complex reality. Consider Emily, a passionate graphic designer known for delivering outstanding projects.

However, when it comes to organizing her workspace, Emily perpetually delays the task. The myth might label her as lazy, but the truth is that she procrastinates on this particular aspect due to a fear of not meeting her own high standards.

Emily's situation illustrates that procrastination doesn't equate to a lack of industriousness but rather a nuanced relationship with specific tasks.

Myth #3: Delay = Procrastination

Not every delay qualifies as procrastination. Let's meet Jim, a strategic planner in a marketing firm. Jim deliberately delays the execution of certain marketing campaigns until closer to peak engagement times.

This intentional delay enhances the campaign's impact, demonstrating that not all delays stem from avoidance or indecision. Understanding the purpose behind the delay is key to distinguishing between strategic planning and procrastination. Jim's story reminds us that, like time, not every delay is wasted; some are invested for greater returns.

In our tech-driven society, the prevalence of procrastination has reached new heights. The constant connectivity, notifications, and the allure of the digital world contribute to the challenge. Smartphones, hailed as productivity tools, have become epicenters of distraction.

The digital age provides an abundance of entertainment, information, and immediate gratification at our fingertips. Social media, streaming services, and online games present irresistible temptations, creating an environment conducive to procrastination. The struggle against procrastination is amplified as the digital landscape continually evolves.

THE ALLURING WORLD OF DISTRACTIONS

In today's hyperconnected world, distractions are ubiquitous. From the incessant notifications on our smartphones to the captivating allure of social media, we are constantly bombarded with stimuli that vie for our attention.

This abundance of distractions poses a significant challenge to our ability to focus and maintain productivity. It's almost as if our brains are constantly playing tug-of-war, with one side pulling us toward our goals and another pulling us toward instant gratification.

Imagine you're sitting down to work on an important project, determined to make significant progress. You open your laptop, ready to dive in, but before you even type a word, your phone buzzes with a notification. You instinctively reach for it, and before you know it, you're lost in a vortex of social media updates, news articles, and cat videos.

This scenario is all too common, highlighting the insidious nature of distractions. They have a way of creeping in unnoticed, subtly diverting our attention away from the task at hand. And the more we let them, the more they become ingrained in our behavior, leading to a vicious cycle of procrastination and hindered productivity.

DISTRACTIONS, THE PROCRASTINATOR'S BEST FRIEND

Distractions and procrastination are like two peas in a pod. They go hand in hand, feeding off each other in a never-ending cycle of delayed action and unfulfilled potential. When we encounter a task that seems daunting or unpleasant, our minds naturally seek out distractions as a way to escape the discomfort or anxiety associated with it.

This is why we often find ourselves scrolling through social media feeds when we should be working on an important project or watching TV when we should be studying for an exam. Distractions provide a temporary reprieve from the stress of the task. But they ultimately prolong our discomfort and hinder our progress.

Storytime: The Distracted Writer

Once upon a time, there was a writer who was known for her ability to craft captivating stories. But as the world of technology evolved, so did her habits. She found herself becoming increasingly drawn to the allure of social media and the endless stream of online distractions.

At first, she managed to balance her writing with her newfound online indulgences. But as the distractions grew more enticing, her writing productivity began to suffer. She would sit down to write, only to find herself lost in a rabbit hole of cat videos and celebrity gossip.

The more she procrastinated, the more stress and anxiety she felt. The tasks that once seemed manageable now loomed over her, and the writer's confidence began to waver. She felt overwhelmed and discouraged, wondering if she would ever regain her ability to focus and write the stories waiting to be told.

STRATEGIES FOR CONQUERING DISTRACTIONS

Overcoming distractions and reclaiming control over our attention is not an easy task. It requires a conscious effort to break free from the patterns that have become deeply ingrained in our behavior. But with determination and the right strategies, we can overcome these challenges and achieve our goals.

The Distraction-Procrastination Nexus: Breaking the Chain

Distractions and procrastination often engage in a symbiotic dance. One feeds into the other, creating a loop that derails productivity. So, how do we break this chain and reclaim our focus?

1. The Power of Prioritization

Strategic prioritization serves as a shield against distractions. Begin by categorizing tasks based on urgency and importance. Tackling high-priority tasks first minimizes the impact of potential distractions, allowing you to focus on critical objectives before the siren call of interruptions grows louder.

The first step to overcoming distractions is identifying the stimuli that trigger your procrastination tendencies. Is it the constant buzz of your phone? The allure of social media? Or the temptation to check the latest news? Once you know your triggers, you can start to develop strategies to avoid or minimize them.

2. The Digital Detox Dance

Our digital devices, while invaluable, are notorious sources of distraction. Harness the power of intentional digital detox periods. Turn off non-essential notifications, create dedicated work zones free from electronic temptations, and consider adopting productivity apps designed to limit your digital dalliances during focused work periods.

While technology can be a distraction, it can also be a solution. Explore apps and tools designed to enhance focus, such as website blockers, task management apps, and ambient noise generators that create a conducive work environment.

3. Sanctuary of Silence

Creating a designated workspace or adopting noise-canceling headphones can transform your environment into a sanctuary of silence. This intentional act of minimizing auditory distractions enhances your ability to concentrate on the task at hand, effectively mitigating the allure of external stimuli.

Embrace mindfulness techniques to anchor your attention in the present moment. Simple practices like deep breathing or a brief meditation session can reset your focus and minimize the impact of external distractions.

4. Time Blocking Brilliance

As explored in the previous chapter, time blocking again proves its efficacy. Allocate specific time blocks for tasks and commit to minimizing potential distractions during these periods. Embrace the discipline of dedicating focused attention to the task within the designated time frame.

5. The Pomodoro Pause

The Pomodoro Technique (as discussed previously) features structured work intervals and timed breaks. In essence, it acts as a distraction-busting ally. By breaking your work into manageable intervals, this technique not only enhances focus but also provides designated moments to address potential distractions during brief pauses.

In addition to this, your workspace should be a haven for focused work, free from clutter and potential distractions. Put away your phone, close unnecessary browser tabs, and let others know that you need uninterrupted time. Consider using noise-canceling headphones or earplugs if you work in a noisy environment.

6. The Art of Saying "No"

Sometimes, the most potent tool against distractions is a simple "no." Politely decline non-urgent requests or invitations during dedicated work periods. Setting boundaries communicates the importance of your focused time and establishes a distraction-resistant perimeter.

As you go through the *vast* sea of stimuli, armed with an understanding of distractions and the strategies to combat them, you can mold yourself toward heightened productivity with a little mindfulness.

Distractions cease to be adversaries and transform into what they're supposed to be, harmonizing with our focus rather than derailing it.

BEATING PROCRASTINATION EFFECTIVELY

There is no doubt that procrastination is the perennial foe of productivity. It sneaks into our lives, delaying tasks and undermining our potential. But there are science-backed strategies that allow you to conquer procrastination and reclaim control over your time. Let's dive into these techniques that empower you to block out distractions, stay focused, and resist the siren call of procrastination.

1. Admit You're Procrastinating (And Try to Understand Why)

The first step in overcoming any challenge is acknowledgment, and procrastination is no exception. According to the McGraw Center for Teaching and Learning at Princeton University, admitting that you're procrastinating is crucial.

Take a moment to reflect on why you're delaying the task. Is it fear of failure, lack of interest, or feeling overwhelmed? Understanding the root cause empowers you to effectively tailor your approach to conquer procrastination.

2. Reverse Pychyl's Procrastination Triggers

Timothy A. Pychyl, a renowned psychologist, has identified specific triggers contributing to procrastination. As highlighted in the Harvard Business Review, these triggers include expectancy, value, time, impulsiveness, and delay.

Understanding and reversing these triggers form a critical strategy. For instance, enhance the value of the task by connecting it to your long-term goals or break it into smaller, more manageable segments to reduce the perceived time commitment.

A few years ago, I found myself entangled in the procrastination web, struggling to complete a challenging research paper during university. The task loomed over me like an insurmountable mountain, triggering a cascade of procrastination triggers. Now that I know of them, I see them as the same ones psychologist Timothy A. Pychyl identified.

Expectancy, the first of Pychyl's triggers, had me doubting my ability to produce a quality paper. The value of the task seemed diminished as my short-term focus overshadowed the long-term benefits. Time, impulsiveness, and delay danced around me, creating a perfect storm of procrastination.

One day, determined to escape this cycle, I decided to reverse the triggers consciously. Instead of viewing the research paper as an overwhelming monolith, I connected it to my long-term goal of academic excellence. I envisioned the sense of accomplishment and the knowledge gained, rekindling the value of the task. Now, I understand that this was me reversing Pychyl's triggers.

Breaking the paper into smaller, manageable segments became my strategy to combat the perceived time commitment. I set achievable milestones, each contributing to the larger goal. This approach not only aligned with Pychyl's insights but also transformed the task into a series of conquerable challenges.

As I progressed through these smaller segments, the expectancy trigger began to shift. With each completed section, my confidence grew, replacing doubt with a sense of capability. The value of the task became increasingly apparent as I witnessed the tangible progress I was making.

Time, once an adversary, transformed into an ally. The impulsiveness that led me astray gave way to a deliberate and structured approach. The delay, which had plagued me before, became a distant memory as I embraced a proactive mindset.

This journey taught me that understanding and reversing procrastination triggers is not just a theoretical concept; it's a practical, transformative strategy. By connecting tasks to long-term goals, breaking them into manageable parts, and reshaping our perception of time, we can explore the threads of procrastination and create a web of productivity.

3. Set Deadlines

Deadlines are powerful motivators that create a sense of urgency. As discussed in a Dataquest article, setting realistic deadlines is a scientifically proven strategy to combat procrastination.

These deadlines act as a guiding force, pushing you to prioritize tasks and allocate your time efficiently. Ensure your deadlines are specific, measurable, and achievable to maximize their effectiveness.

4. Set Immediate Rewards

Immediate rewards serve as incentives to propel you past procrastination's grasp. James Clear, a renowned author and productivity expert, emphasizes the importance of setting immediate rewards.

Celebrate small victories during your tasks, whether it's taking a short break, enjoying a snack, or engaging in a brief activity you enjoy. These mini-rewards create a positive feedback loop, reinforcing the habit of focused work.

5. Set Immediate Consequences

The concept of immediate consequences, highlighted by James Clear, acts as a counterbalance to rewards. Create a system where delaying tasks results in immediate, tangible consequences.

This could involve forfeiting a break, delaying a pleasurable activity, or facing a small penalty. By linking consequences directly to procrastination, you create a powerful deterrent that nudges you toward timely action.

6. Address Other Factors Influencing Procrastination

Procrastination is often intertwined with factors like fear of failure, lack of clarity, or perfectionism. Addressing these underlying issues is crucial for effective procrastination management.

The Dataquest blog advises tackling perfectionism by embracing the concept of "good enough" and cultivating a growth mindset to overcome the fear of failure.

Consider Lily, for example, a dedicated perfectionist whose pursuit of flawlessness often led to procrastination. Staring at a blank document, paralyzed by the fear of failure, she decided to challenge herself. Inspired by the advice to embrace the "*good enough*" principle, Lily shifted her mindset.

Instead of aiming for unattainable perfection, she set a new goal—to produce satisfactory work that met the basic requirements. This adjustment transformed her fear of failure into a catalyst for improvement. The concept of "*good enough*" became a guiding principle, allowing her to break free from the shackles of procrastination.

Addressing the underlying factor of perfectionism and adopting a growth mindset not only improved Lily's productivity but also infused her work with newfound creativity. By realizing that sometimes, good enough is not just sufficient—it's liberating, Lily conquered procrastination and discovered a more fulfilling approach to her tasks.

7. Do Anything to Start

Starting a task is often the most challenging part. The Harvard Business Review advocates the "Do Anything" strategy, emphasizing the importance of initiating the task, even in a minimalistic way. Break the inertia by committing to working on the task for just a few minutes. Once you're in motion, the psychological barriers to continued action diminish, making it easier to sustain focus.

These scientific strategies arm you with the keys to a procrastination-free future. Admitting procrastination, understanding its triggers, and implementing effective techniques empower you to break free from the chains of delay.

Set deadlines, leverage rewards and consequences, and address underlying factors to cultivate a proactive approach to your tasks. As you head on this journey to triumph over procrastination, remember that every small step forward is a victory.

CREATING YOUR OWN FOCUSED LIFESTYLE

In our fast-paced world, maintaining focus can be challenging. But certain lifestyle changes can significantly impact our ability to concentrate and overcome procrastination. Let's explore a few habits that can enhance your focus and productivity:

Sleep More:

- Quality sleep is crucial for cognitive function and concentration. Aim for 7-9 hours of sleep each night to ensure your mind is well-rested and ready for the day's challenges.

Drink More Water:

- Dehydration can lead to fatigue and difficulty in concentrating. Stay hydrated throughout the day by drinking an adequate amount of water. A well-hydrated brain is a focused brain.

Take Up Meditation:

- Incorporating meditation into your daily routine can improve mindfulness and focus. Even a few minutes of meditation each day can make a significant difference in your ability to stay present and attentive.

Take More and Better Breaks:

- Effective breaks can rejuvenate your mind. Refer to the insights from Chapter 2 to ensure that the breaks you take are truly refreshing and contribute to improved focus when you return to your tasks.

Check if You're Multitasking:

- While multitasking might seem like a time-saving strategy, it often leads to reduced focus and productivity. Try focusing on one task at a time to enhance concentration.

Stay in the Present:

- Avoid dwelling on past mistakes or worrying about the future. Practice mindfulness to stay in the present moment, enabling you to tackle tasks with greater clarity.

Create a Bedtime and/or Morning Routine:

- Establishing routines helps signal to your brain that it's time to transition between activities. A consistent bedtime routine can improve the quality of your sleep.

Track Your Energy:

- Pay attention to your energy levels throughout the day. Note when you feel the most energized and productive, and plan your most important tasks during these peak periods.

Do a Digital Detox Regularly:

- Periodically disconnecting from digital devices can reduce distractions and improve your ability to focus. Follow the steps outlined in the previous chapter for a successful digital detox.

Get More Physical Activity In:

- Regular exercise has numerous cognitive benefits, including improved focus and reduced stress. Incorporate physical activity into your routine to boost your overall well-being.

Here's a table you can use to mark the completion of each milestone.

Lifestyle Change	Implementation Status
Sleep More	
Drink More Water	
Take Up Meditation	
Take More and Better Breaks	
Check if You're Multitasking	
Stay in the Present	
Create a Bedtime Routine	
Track Your Energy	
Do a Digital Detox Regularly	
Get More Physical Activity In	

Procrastination is a universal challenge, and understanding its nuances is the first step toward overcoming it. As we've looked into the various facets of procrastination, it's crucial to reiterate that the common myths surrounding it—linking procrastination to laziness or a lack of willpower—are often oversimplified. Procrastination is a complex interplay of psychological factors, and the strategies we've explored aim to navigate this landscape.

Remember, admitting you're procrastinating is not a sign of weakness; it's an opportunity for growth. It's not about lacking willpower or laziness but understanding the deeper motivations behind your actions. Embracing science-backed techniques, addressing underlying issues, and making intentional lifestyle changes can significantly impact your ability to beat procrastination.

As we move forward, keep in mind that each individual is unique, and the journey to overcoming procrastination is a personal one. Experiment with the strategies provided, and don't be discouraged if it takes time to find what works best for you. The key is to persist and celebrate the small victories along the way.

With a clearer understanding of procrastination and armed with effective tools, you're better equipped to face the challenges of managing your time. In the next part of this book, we'll focus on the specific hurdles students often encounter in their quest for effective time management. Get ready to explore practical solutions to real-world obstacles and take the next step toward a more organized and productive academic journey.

7

SCHOOL VS. EXTRACURRICULARS

"Your life, time, and brain should belong to you, not to an institution."

— GRACE LLEWELLYN

In the whirlwind of academic responsibilities and extracurricular pursuits, finding the delicate balance between school commitments and outside interests can feel like walking a tightrope. Grace Llewellyn's words resonate, reminding us that our lives are not meant to be solely dictated by institutions but shaped by our passions, interests, and personal growth.

As students, the journey through academia is not just about acing exams or completing assignments; it's a holistic experience that encompasses personal development, exploration, and the pursuit of one's interests beyond the classroom walls. Extracurricular activities offer a gateway to a world beyond textbooks, providing opportunities to hone diverse skills, foster leadership qualities, and build a well-rounded personality.

However, the challenge lies in the delicate art of balancing academic demands with the allure of extracurricular pursuits. This chapter aims to be your guide through the labyrinth of school and extracurricular activities, offering insights, strategies, and practical tips to help you not only navigate but thrive in both realms.

I understand the dichotomy you face – the desire to excel academically while exploring passions outside the academic sphere. I struggled with it for quite some time before finding the perfect balance. But by then, I only had a year left before graduating. My goal is to help you learn from my experiences and make the most out of school and extracurricular activities concurrently.

THE IMPORTANCE OF EXTRACURRICULAR ACTIVITIES

When I started college, the first piece of advice I received wasn't about acing exams or navigating the campus—it was about the importance of getting involved in extracurricular activities. It wasn't just a suggestion to fill my schedule but a roadmap to enrich my overall college experience.

Little did I know that beyond the classrooms and text-books, these activities would shape not only my time management skills but also equip me with invaluable life skills.

Extracurricular activities come in various forms—sports, clubs, additional classes for hobbies or skills—and each offers a unique set of merits. Beyond the obvious physical and mental health benefits, engaging in extracurriculars introduces a dynamic element to your routine, teaching you how to juggle different responsibilities and manage your time effectively.

Communication & Collaboration

One of the most significant advantages of participating in extracurricular activities is the opportunity to develop essential life skills, with communication and collaboration taking center stage. These skills extend far beyond the confines of the activity itself, proving instrumental in academic pursuits, future careers, and personal relationships.

1. Active Listening

In the noise of modern life, active listening has become a rare skill. Engaging in activities that involve teamwork or group dynamics hones this skill. This is particularly true for the digital-first world we live in today. Ads and distracting YouTube videos, TikTok, Snapchat, Instagram, and other social media platforms are primary examples of this.

Whether you're a member of a debate club or part of a sports team, active listening ensures that you grasp the nuances of different perspectives, a skill invaluable in academic discussions and workplace collaborations.

2. Using Clear Language

Clarity in communication is a hallmark of effective leaders. Extracurricular activities provide a platform to practice articulating thoughts and ideas clearly. Whether you're explaining a strategy in a sports match or presenting a proposal in a club meeting, the ability to use clear language fosters understanding and cooperation.

Let's say you're part of a debate club, and the topic for the day is environmental conservation. Your task is to present a proposal for implementing a recycling program in your school. Here's how using clear language plays a crucial role:

In this scenario, using clear language involves breaking down the proposal into concise and understandable points. Instead of using jargon or complex terminology, you focus on conveying the importance of recycling, the specific steps involved, and the anticipated benefits for the school community.

By articulating your thoughts clearly, you ensure that every club member understands the proposal, fostering a shared understanding that is essential for collaboration and support. This skill is transferable to countless situations, from explaining ideas in the classroom to presenting projects in the workplace.

3. Face-to-Face Communication

In an era dominated by digital communication, face-to-face interaction remains a powerful skill. Joining clubs or groups that encourage in-person discussions helps break down communication barriers. This skill becomes a significant asset in job interviews, networking events, and any scenario where personal connection matters.

Let's say you're part of a drama club, and your group is preparing for a live performance. Face-to-face communication is vital during rehearsals. You need to express your ideas about character development, coordinate with fellow actors on stage movements, and provide instant feedback.

This in-person interaction not only enhances the overall quality of the performance but also builds strong interpersonal skills that are invaluable in real-world situations like job interviews or networking events.

4. Tone Usage

Understanding the nuances of tone in communication is crucial. In the context of extracurriculars, especially those involving leadership roles, you'll find yourself navigating diverse personalities. Mastering tone usage helps convey authority, empathy, or collaboration, depending on the situation.

5. Nonverbal Communication

They say actions speak louder than words, and nonverbal cues often convey more than verbal expressions. Engaging in activities where nonverbal communication is key, such as theater or dance, refines your ability to express ideas, emotions, and intentions without uttering a word.

As you focus on these skills through extracurricular activities, remember that they are not confined to the realm of the activity itself. They are tools that will serve you well in your academic pursuits, professional endeavors, and personal relationships.

Practice them consciously, and you'll find yourself not only excelling in your chosen activities but also becoming a more effective communicator and collaborator in all aspects of life.

BALANCING STRATEGIES

Balancing academics and extracurricular activities is a juggling act, but mastering this skill early on can set the stage for a more organized and fulfilling future. As you dive into the realm of academic pursuits and engage in various extracurricular projects, it's essential to strike a balance that not only ensures success in your studies but also allows you to excel in your chosen activities outside the classroom.

Numerous strategies can help you navigate this delicate equilibrium. These approaches not only enhance your current academic and extracurricular experiences but also lay the foundation for effective time management in your future endeavors.

Let's explore some valuable strategies that will empower you to gracefully manage both fronts:

Prioritize Your Commitments

Understanding the importance and time requirements of each commitment is the first step toward effective balance. Consider the deadlines, significance, and personal goals associated with your academic and extracurricular tasks.

For example, if you have a major project due in a week and a club meeting the next day, prioritize completing the project first. This approach allows you to direct your energy and attention to what truly matters at any given moment, ensuring you meet your obligations efficiently.

Create a Realistic Schedule

Developing a realistic schedule is essential for harmonizing academic and extracurricular responsibilities.

When crafting your timetable, be honest about the time each task demands. If you have a heavy academic workload, allocate sufficient time for studying and assignments.

Simultaneously, ensure there are dedicated slots for your extracurricular activities. A well-structured schedule prevents last-minute rushes and reduces stress. For instance, schedule study sessions during your most productive hours and reserve evenings for club meetings or sports practice.

Learn to Say No

As mentioned in the previous chapter, while embracing challenges is commendable, recognizing your limits is equally important. Learn to say no when additional commitments may compromise the quality of your work or your well-being.

Suppose a friend invites you to join a new club, but you're already juggling academics and a leadership role in another organization. Politely declining allows you to maintain the quality of your existing commitments and avoids spreading yourself too thin.

Efficient Time Management Techniques

Embracing time management techniques tailored to your preferences enhances productivity. For instance, if you find the Pomodoro Technique effective, allocate focused study sessions with short breaks in between.

If time blocking resonates with you, allocate specific blocks for academic tasks and extracurricular activities. Experiment with different methods to discover what works best for you, which can significantly boost your efficiency.

Establish Clear Goals

Setting clear, achievable goals for academic and extracurricular pursuits provides a roadmap for success. If you're part of a science club, set a goal for completing a challenging experiment by the end of the month.

Similarly, establish academic goals, such as achieving a certain GPA. Regularly reassess these goals to ensure they remain relevant and attainable, adjusting them as needed based on your evolving priorities and aspirations.

Communication is Key

Effective communication with teachers, peers, and colleagues involved in your activities is vital. Keep them informed about your schedule and commitments, fostering understanding and support.

If you have a major exam approaching and need additional study time, communicate this to your extracurricular team. Open lines of communication contribute to a supportive environment, allowing for better collaboration and shared success.

Utilize Downtime Effectively

Maximize your downtime by incorporating small tasks or study sessions. For example, if you're waiting for a club meeting to start, use that time to review class notes or plan your next academic move.

Turning pockets of downtime into productive moments ensures that you make the most of your day without feeling overwhelmed by constant multitasking. This approach helps you maintain a steady academic and extracurricular rhythm, contributing to a more balanced and fulfilling lifestyle.

Remember, the art of balancing academics and extracurriculars is a skill that evolves over time. It's not about finding a perfect balance every day but adapting to changing circumstances and staying dedicated to your overall growth and development.

As you embrace academic challenges and extracurricular pursuits, you're not just managing time but *shaping a lifestyle that prepares you for a successful future.*

THE DANGERS OF BURNOUT: NAVIGATING THE THIN LINE

Engaging in extracurricular activities can be a rewarding experience, providing students with opportunities to learn, grow, and connect with peers. However, when these activities accumulate, especially during demanding academic periods, the risk of burnout becomes a genuine concern.

Burnout is not merely feeling drained; it is a comprehensive state of physical, mental, and emotional exhaustion resulting from chronic stress and overwork.

Understanding the 5 Stages of Burnout

To comprehend the severity of burnout, exploring the stages that lead to this detrimental state is crucial. The 5 Stages of Burnout, as outlined in various studies, provide insights into the progression of this phenomenon.

1. Honeymoon Phase: Enthusiastic Beginnings

In the Honeymoon Phase, students start their extracurricular journey with boundless enthusiasm. Take David, for instance, a second-year high school student. Eager to explore interests beyond academics, David joins the school newspaper.

The initial days are marked by excitement, fueled by the opportunity to contribute creatively. Writing articles and attending meetings are seen as invigorating challenges rather than burdens.

2. Onset of Stress: The Rising Tide

As David invests himself further into the responsibilities of being a journalist, the Onset of Stress begins to emerge. The demands of meeting deadlines, conducting interviews, and balancing academic commitments start to take a toll.

David notices a rise in fatigue but dismisses it, attributing it to the inevitable challenges of a busy schedule. The stress is considered a normal part of the journey, and the initial passion keeps David moving forward.

3. Chronic Stress: Balancing on the Tightrope

As demands intensify, stress transforms into Chronic Stress. David experiences persistent fatigue, and academic performance starts to waver. Balancing the relationship between writing articles, attending classes, and managing personal time becomes increasingly challenging.

Chronic stress leads to moments of irritability and frustration. Yet, the commitment to the newspaper persists, overshadowing the toll it's taking.

4. Burnout: The Breaking Point

In the Burnout stage, David reaches a critical juncture. Physical and mental well-being experience a significant decline. Exhaustion permeates every aspect of life. Tasks that once brought joy now feel like insurmountable burdens.

Writing articles, once a source of pride, becomes a daunting obligation. Burnout casts a dark shadow over David's passion, leaving a pervasive sense of emptiness.

5. Habitual Burnout: The Inescapable Routine

In the final stage, Burnout becomes ingrained in David's lifestyle, transitioning into Habitual Burnout. Physical and emotional symptoms intensify, creating a cycle that feels impossible to break.

Now, David finds it challenging to recover, and the once-thriving extracurricular activity has become a relentless source of stress. The joy initially accompanying the endeavor has been replaced by a perpetual sense of overwhelm.

Navigating Burnout: Breaking the Cycle

David's journey through the stages of burnout highlights the importance of recognizing the signs early on. By acknowledging the risks, implementing effective coping mechanisms, and seeking support, students can prevent burnout from becoming a habitual part of their lives.

The key lies in fostering a balance between academic and extracurricular pursuits while prioritizing mental and physical well-being.

POTENTIAL TRIGGERS OF BURNOUT

Navigating the delicate balance between academics and extracurriculars exposes students to various triggers that can lead to burnout. Understanding these triggers is crucial for implementing preventive measures and fostering a healthy equilibrium in a student's life.

1. Overcommitment: Striking a Delicate Balance

Overcommitment is a prominent trigger, luring students into the trap of taking on too many responsibilities without considering personal limits. The initial excitement of involvement can transform into overwhelming stress if not met with prudent planning and a realistic assessment of one's capacity.

2. Perfectionism: The Pursuit of the Unattainable

The relentless pursuit of perfection, whether in academics or extracurriculars, creates a breeding ground for burnout. Students driven by an unyielding quest for flawlessness may find themselves trapped in a cycle of self-imposed pressure, pushing the boundaries of their mental and emotional resilience.

3. Lack of Support: The Weight of Isolation

Insufficient support, be it from peers, mentors, or family members, contributes significantly to the burden of burnout. Feeling isolated in the face of mounting responsibilities amplifies stress. Establishing a robust support network becomes imperative for students to navigate challenges without succumbing to the weight of isolation.

4. Inadequate Rest: Balancing the Sleep Equation

A consistent lack of sleep and relaxation adds fuel to the burnout fire. Physical and mental fatigue, resulting from inadequate rest, heightens the challenges of managing academic and extracurricular commitments. Prioritizing rest becomes a foundational aspect of maintaining well-being in the demands of a student's multifaceted life.

EFFECTS OF BURNOUT ON PHYSICAL, MENTAL, AND EMOTIONAL HEALTH

Understanding the negative consequences of burnout is essential for students striving to maintain a healthy balance. Burnout can manifest in various ways, impacting not only academic performance but also overall well-being.

Physical Effects:

- Persistent fatigue
- Sleep disturbances
- Weakened immune system
- Headaches and muscle tension

Mental Effects:

- Cognitive decline
- Difficulty concentrating
- Memory issues
- Increased negativity and cynicism

Emotional Effects:

- Emotional exhaustion
- Decreased sense of accomplishment
- Feelings of detachment
- Increased irritability and frustration

RECOGNIZING THE EARLY WARNING SIGNS OF BURNOUT

Burnout usually takes some time to manifest. There is a very good chance that as you repeat something over and over, you'll start feeling some symptoms of an onset of burnout - no matter how much you love what you're doing.

Here are some early warning signs of burnout onset to keep in mind:

Loss of Interest in Once-Enjoyed Activities

The initial warning sign of burnout often manifests as a Loss of Interest in activities that were once a source of joy. Michelle, an avid painter, may notice a diminishing passion for her art. The paintings that used to be a form of self-expression may now start feeling like burdens, leading her to question the very activities that once brought fulfillment.

Chronic Fatigue and Low Energy Levels

A pervasive sense of fatigue and consistently low energy levels characterize the onset of burnout. Stan, a dedicated soccer player, may find himself struggling to summon the usual enthusiasm for practice and matches.

The energy that fueled his passion for the game may become elusive after a while, replaced by a lingering tiredness that transcends physical exertion.

Decline in Academic Performance

Burnout doesn't discriminate—it affects various facets of life, including academic performance. Emma, for example, who was an ambitious student involved in multiple extracurriculars, may start witnessing a decline in her grades.

The once-sharp focus on assignments and exams may start getting replaced by a mental fog, impacting her ability to excel academically.

Increased Feelings of Frustration and Irritability

The emotional toll of burnout surfaces in heightened feelings of frustration and irritability. Henry, a dedicated volunteer, for example, may start noticing a shift in his demeanor. Tasks that were once approached with enthusiasm now evoke irritation.

The emotional strain of balancing commitments may end up manifesting in subtle yet impactful changes in behavior that others may start noticing first.

Difficulty Concentrating & Making Decisions

As burnout progresses, cognitive functions are affected, leading to difficulty concentrating and making decisions. Consider the example of Julia, who is usually actively engaged in various leadership roles. She may start experiencing mental fog over time.

Once adept at making informed decisions, she may start grappling with uncertainty and indecisiveness, further contributing to her feeling overwhelmed.

STRATEGIES FOR BURNOUT PREVENTION & RECOVERY

Once you start seeing these signs or notice that you are burned out, there are several key strategies that you can adopt. While it is a good idea to distance yourself from the burnout-causing activity, it is neither a lasting solution nor the only part of the solution.

Here are some things you can do to prevent and recover from burnout:

Establishing Boundaries: Defining Your Limits

Setting clear boundaries on commitments is paramount to prevent burnout. Continuing the example of David, a student balancing academics and a part-time job, he may learn to articulate his limits. By delineating the scope of his responsibilities, he avoids overextension, ensuring a more sustainable balance between work and personal life.

Prioritizing Self-Care: Nurturing Well-Being

In the demands of academics and extracurriculars, prioritizing self-care becomes a cornerstone of burnout prevention. David may start allocating dedicated time for rest and rejuvenation. Engaging in activities that bring joy and relaxation will safeguard his mental and emotional well-being.

Seeking Support: Building a Support System

Acknowledging the need for support is a crucial step in burnout prevention. David may choose to reach out to friends and mentors. Establishing open lines of communication fosters understanding and will provide a valuable support system during demanding times.

Reevaluating Goals: Ensuring Alignment with Well-Being

Regularly reassessing academic and extracurricular goals is essential for preventing burnout. David may take some time off to reflect on his aspirations again. By ensuring that his goals align with his overall well-being, he can cultivate a sense of purpose and avoid the pitfalls of burnout.

CHECKLIST: CHOOSING THE RIGHT EXTRACURRICULAR ACTIVITY

Starting your journey of selecting an extracurricular activity can be both exciting and challenging. The right choice can enhance your high school experience, offering opportunities for personal growth, skill development, and community engagement.

To assist you in making an informed decision, use the checklist below. Evaluate each factor to ensure the chosen activity aligns with your interests, schedule, and overall well-being.

Criteria	Consideration	Yes/No
Does it Cater to Your Interests or Talents?	Identify activities that resonate with your passions and skills.	
Is It Nearby?	Consider the proximity of the activity to your home or school.	
Is It in a Safe Environment?	Prioritize activities held in secure environments.	
Are Trusted Adults Supervising It?	Ensure responsible and trustworthy adults oversee the activity.	
Is It Accredited/Sponsored by the School?	Reflects positively on your commitment to school-supported initiatives.	
Is It Within Budget?	Assess potential costs for materials or equipment.	
Do You Know Anyone in the Club/Organization?	Acquaintances can make the experience more enjoyable.	
Is It Something You've Done Before?	Consider your familiarity for comfort and confidence.	
Can You Balance It With Your Current Workload?	Ensure a harmonious balance with academic commitments.	
Is It Something You Can Realistically Travel to and Participate in With Your Current Schedule?	Be practical about logistics and feasibility.	

Evaluate each criterion based on your preferences and circumstances, keeping in mind that the goal is to find an extracurricular activity that enhances your high school journey. The checklist serves as a comprehensive guide to support your decision-making process, ensuring a rewarding and enriching experience.

In the delicate dance between academics and extracurricular activities, *finding balance is essential for mastering your hobbies, study, and life.* As we navigate the myriad of choices and commitments, it's essential to remember that pursuing excellence should not come at the cost of well-being. We've looked at the importance of extracurricular activities, exploring how they can shape not just academic skills but also crucial life skills such as communication and time management.

However, spotlighting these endeavors comes with a cautionary tale—the looming risk of burnout. We've discussed the stages and perils of burnout, emphasizing the necessity of recognizing its early signs and implementing preventive strategies. Yet, our journey is far from over.

The next chapter will illuminate this subject even further, providing insights into the world of academics, extracurriculars, and the delicate equilibrium required to flourish without succumbing to exhaustion. As we focus on the nuanced discussion of burnout, remember that our goal is not just success in academics and activities but the holistic well-being of every teenager navigating this challenging yet transformative phase of life.

8

CHAPTER 8:STRESS VS. SCHEDULING

"Stress is like a rocking chair—it gives you something to do but gets you nowhere."

— GLENN TURNER

Stress often plays an unwelcome but all-too-familiar role in teenage life. As we step into the world of stress and scheduling, statistics show that there has recently been a significant uptick in anxiety and depression diagnoses among children aged 3 to 17.

This chapter serves as a cautionary tale and a guiding light, delving into the perils of stress, continuing the conversation on burnout from the previous chapter, and equipping you with the tools to recognize, manage, and ultimately overcome the challenges that stress presents.

Our exploration will discuss the balance between stress and scheduling, illuminating the subtle yet profound impact on physical, mental, and emotional well-being. Beyond the alarming statistics lies the understanding that stress is not merely a byproduct of a hectic lifestyle but a force that, if left unchecked, can disrupt the delicate equilibrium teenagers strive to maintain.

In my teenage years, stress wasn't a distant concept; it was a relentless companion, weaving its presence into the tapestry of my daily life. I distinctly remember the pressure mounting as academic deadlines collided with extracurricular commitments, creating a perfect storm of stress. It wasn't just about getting through the day but navigating a maze of expectations, societal pressures, and the constant hum of impending responsibilities.

One memory stands out—a late-night study session fueled by caffeine and the looming specter of exams. The weight of expectations bore down, and stress became an uninvited guest, settling into the room like a heavy fog. In that moment, the challenges felt insurmountable, and the idea of balancing everything seemed like an impossible feat.

Reflecting on those times, it is now clear to me that stress isn't just an external force but a deeply personal experience shaping the narrative of our teenage years.

UNDERSTANDING THE SIGNS & SYMPTOMS OF STRESS IN TEENAGE YEARS

In the rollercoaster of adolescence, stress emerges as an unexpected but prevalent companion, affecting teenagers in ways that might not always be immediately apparent. Recent studies, such as those highlighted by developmental science and the American Academy of Pediatrics, emphasize the escalating levels of stress among teens. As we look into the basics of recognizing stress in teenagers, it's essential to bridge the gap between statistical trends and individual experiences.

Stress in teenagers often manifests in subtle yet impactful ways. Sources from UNICEF, the American Psychological Association (APA), and Verywell Mind outline common indicators that signal heightened stress levels in teens. These signs can range from emotional shifts and changes in behavior to physical symptoms like headaches or fatigue.

Recognizing these indicators is crucial for teenagers and those who support them. Here's a comprehensive look at the signs and symptoms of stress in the teenage years:

1. Emotional Changes:

- Mood Swings: Rapid shifts in mood, from moments of elation to periods of irritability or sadness.

- Increased Anxiety: Persistent worry, fear, or nervousness that goes beyond the usual teenage concerns.

2. Behavioral Shifts:

- Changes in Sleep Patterns: Insomnia, frequent waking during the night, or oversleeping.
- Appetite Changes: Significant weight loss or gain due to changes in eating habits.
- Withdrawal: Social isolation, reluctance to participate in activities once enjoyed, or avoiding social interactions.

3. Physical Symptoms:

- Headaches: Unexplained or tension-related headaches that become recurrent.
- Fatigue: Constant feelings of tiredness or lack of energy, even after sufficient rest.
- Stomach Issues: Digestive problems, including nausea, stomachaches, or changes in bowel habits.

4. Academic Challenges:

- Decline in Performance: A noticeable drop in academic achievement or a sudden disinterest in school.

- Procrastination: Difficulty initiating tasks or consistently putting off assignments.

5. Behavioral Changes:

- Irritability: Heightened irritability or a short temper, often over minor issues.
- Unexplained Aches and Pains: Physical complaints without an apparent medical cause.
- Changes in Personal Habits: Alterations in personal hygiene or routines.

6. Psychological Indicators:

- Difficulty Concentrating: Inability to focus on tasks or concentrate on academic assignments.
- Memory Issues: Forgetfulness or difficulty recalling information.
- Increased Self-Criticism: A rise in negative self-talk and harsh self-evaluation.

Reflecting on my teenage years, I clearly recall moments when stress subtly infiltrated my daily life, leaving its imprint on my physical and emotional well-being. These signs, though varied, served as valuable indicators that stress was exerting its influence.

The ability to recognize these signals, coupled with open communication, lays the foundation for proactive stress management—a skill that proves invaluable as teenagers navigate the complexities of adolescence.

HOW STRESS AFFECTS TEENS

Stress, often dismissed as a normal part of adolescence, can wield a profound impact on teenagers across various dimensions—physically, mentally, and emotionally. Understanding these effects is essential for both teens and those who guide them.

Let's take a look at some ways stress shapes the teenage experience:.

Physical Toll

Stress disrupts sleep patterns, contributing to insomnia or irregular sleep, further exacerbating fatigue, and impacting overall well-being. Elevated stress levels can also lead to stomachaches, nausea, or other digestive problems, highlighting the mind-body connection.

Mental Strain

High stress levels linked to academic expectations can hinder cognitive function, impeding memory, concentration, and the ability to process information effectively.

Furthermore, chronic stress is a known precursor to anxiety and depression in teens, emphasizing the importance of early recognition and intervention.

Emotional Impact

Stress contributes to emotional turbulence, causing abrupt shifts in mood, ranging from irritability to feelings of sadness or hopelessness. As stress intensifies, teens may withdraw from social activities, affecting interpersonal relationships and amplifying feelings of isolation.

Cognitive Consequences

The cognitive toll of stress can impede a teen's ability to make informed decisions, affecting their judgment and problem-solving skills. Chronic stress may also foster negative self-talk and self-perception, influencing a teen's sense of identity and self-worth.

Behavioral Responses

Teens under stress may exhibit behavioral changes, including increased irritability, impulsivity, or social withdrawal. These responses are adaptive mechanisms that signal the need for support and coping strategies.

Coping Mechanisms

Under stress, teens may resort to unhealthy coping mechanisms such as substance abuse, self-harm, or disordered eating, attempting to manage overwhelming emotions.

Understanding these dimensions of stress equips teens and their support systems with the knowledge needed to identify early signs and implement effective coping mechanisms. This awareness fosters an environment where teens can openly address and manage stress, ensuring a healthier transition into adulthood.

STRESS MANAGEMENT: GOING THROUGH LIFE'S STORMS

Stress management is like having a toolkit for life's challenges. It's not about making stress disappear (because, let's face it, that's impossible). But it's about having strategies to deal with it.

The World Health Organization, which is like the superhero of health advice, says stress management is super important. Newport Academy, a group of mental health experts, adds that it's not just about avoiding stress but taking care of our overall mental health.

Coping Techniques:

Now, let's talk about some cool tools you can put in your stress management toolkit. Think of these like karate moves that help you stay strong when stress tries to knock you down:

Mindfulness & Relaxation Techniques: Hit Pause on Stress

Imagine stress being a wild beast, and you have a magical remote control that can make it freeze. That's what mindfulness, deep breathing, and yoga do—they hit the pause button.

Mindfulness is paying full attention to the present moment without judgment. It's like momentarily stopping time, letting you catch your breath. Deep breathing is your superpower against stress.

It slows your heartbeat and calms your mind. And yoga? It's a superhero pose that makes stress retreat. Together, they create a shield against the chaos, helping you regain control.

My brother and I found ourselves stressed quite often during my teen years. Our father noticed us out of our minds but never said anything about it. Perhaps this was his way of giving us our space, but it had another unintended consequence, too.

We both took inspiration from him, seeing how he would remain calm even under the most dire circumstances. We once saw him in a traffic argument, and he managed to diffuse the tension without raising his voice. His mindfulness eventually transferred to us, which turned out to be a huge help in managing stress for us siblings.

Expressive Writing: The Secret Diary of Stress Relief

Stress can feel like a tangled mess of thoughts and emotions. Imagine having a magic diary where you pour out your feelings; suddenly, everything becomes clearer and lighter.

That's the power of expressive writing. It's not about perfect grammar or spelling but letting your thoughts flow onto paper. This superhero move is your secret weapon, exploring the knots of stress and turning them into a story you can understand and conquer.

Physical Activity: Train Like a Stress-Fighting Superhero

Envision yourself as a superhero in training. Regular exercise is your cape, and your sneakers are your power boots. It's not just about staying physically fit; it's about releasing those magical happy chemicals in your brain.

When you move, stress trembles and retreats. Whether it's a jog, a dance, or a game, physical activity is your superhero training ground, making you resilient and strong against the stress invaders.

Positive Social Connections: Your Stress-Busting Squad

In the superhero world, every hero has a team. In your stress-fighting journey, your friends and family are that squad. They're not just there for the good times; they're your support system when stress hits hard.

Talking to them is like activating a shield that protects you from the chaos. They lend an understanding ear and share wisdom; sometimes, just being around them can be the antidote to stress. Your positive social connections are the backbone of your stress-busting squad, ready to tackle anything together.

Time Management Techniques: Master the Art of Time-Turning

Ever wish you had a time-turner like Hermione from Harry Potter? While time-turners might be fictional, time management techniques are the real deal.

The Pomodoro Technique, for instance, is like having a time-turner in your hands. As mentioned in a previous chapter, it's a strategy where you work for a set period, then take a short break.

This technique helps you manage your time efficiently, keeping stress at bay. By mastering time management, you become the wizard of your schedule, making stress disappear like magic.

Creative Outlets: Unlock Your Stress-Relief Superpower

What's your superpower? Drawing, singing, or playing an instrument? Your creative side is a stress-relief superpower waiting to be unlocked. It's not about being the next Picasso or Mozart; it's about expressing yourself freely.

Drawing can be your superhero cape, music your shield, and creativity your weapon against stress. Engaging in creative outlets helps you channel your emotions positively, turning stress into art and making you feel awesome in the process.

Problem-Solving Skills: Become the Architect of Solutions

Imagine you're an architect designing a solution to escape the stress maze. Problem-solving skills are your blueprint. Break down big problems into smaller, manageable parts.

Identify possible solutions and weigh their pros and cons. It's like constructing a stress-free path, brick by brick.

With each solution, you build a bridge to walk confidently through the maze.

For example, during my high school years, the looming challenge of choosing the right college felt like an insurmountable maze. It was a rather stressful decision - no doubt. Instead of succumbing to the stress, I applied problem-solving skills.

Breaking down the overwhelming decision into smaller parts, I identified factors that mattered most to me—academic programs, campus culture, and location. By weighing the pros and cons of each option, it was like constructing a bridge of clarity within the maze of uncertainty.

Ultimately, this approach led me to confidently navigate the complex decision-making process and choose the college that aligned with my goals and values.

Assertiveness: Your Shield Against Unnecessary Stress

Picture yourself with a superhero shield that deflects unnecessary stress. That shield is assertiveness. Assertiveness isn't about being aggressive or passive; it's finding the middle ground.

It's expressing your thoughts and feelings clearly and respectfully. When you communicate assertively, stress encounters a powerful barrier, leaving you in control of your boundaries and emotions.

Humor as a Stress-Busting Sidekick

Stress can be a formidable opponent, but humor is your witty sidekick. Laughter has the power to lighten the heaviest of burdens. It releases endorphins, your body's natural stress reliever.

So, don't hesitate to find the humor in everyday situations. Whether it's a funny meme, a silly joke, or a moment of playful laughter, let humor be your trusty sidekick in the battle against stress.

Back in high school, facing a mountain of assignments and exams, I decided to take a break and indulge in a moment of stress relief. As a result, I chose to help my mother bake cookies.

Little did I know that my attempt at baking cookies for the first time would turn into a comedy of errors - not just for me but for my family. Mixing sugar with salt and misreading the oven temperature, my kitchen quickly transformed into a battlefield of culinary chaos. In essence, I didn't just mess up my stress relief venture, but my mom's cooking.

The result? A batch of cookies that could double as hockey pucks. As we stared at my kitchen disaster, we couldn't help but burst into laughter at the absurdity of the situation. However, there was a silver lining. While my stress relief session wasn't as successful, the humor ended up refreshing me much more than unexpected!

Mindfulness Meditation: The Zen Warrior's Secret

Close your eyes and imagine becoming a Zen warrior equipped with the power of mindfulness meditation. Mindfulness is about being present in the moment without judgment.

Meditation helps you tame the chaos in your mind, creating a tranquil space. Regular practice enhances your ability to stay calm in stressful situations. It's like having a meditation sword that cuts through stress, leaving you centered and focused.

Building a Support System: Your Stress-Resilient Tribe

In the realm of stress, your support system is your tribe. Surround yourself with people who uplift and understand you. Share your thoughts, fears, and triumphs with trusted friends, family, or mentors.

This tribe becomes your stronghold, offering encouragement and advice. By building a robust support system, you're not navigating the maze alone. You have allies cheering you on, making the journey through stress more manageable and less daunting.

SELF-REFLECTION CHECKLIST: ASSESS YOUR STRESS LEVELS

Take a moment to reflect on your own experiences and feelings. This checklist will help you identify signs of stress and areas where you can implement stress management strategies.

Self-Reflection Checklist: Assess Your Stress Levels	Description	Check
1. Emotional Check	• Are you experiencing frequent mood swings? • Do you find yourself worrying excessively about various aspects of your life?	
2. Behavioral Check	• Have you noticed changes in your sleep patterns or appetite? • Are you withdrawing from social activities that once brought you joy?	
3. Physical Check	• Are you frequently experiencing headaches, fatigue, or stomach issues? • Have you observed unexplained aches or pains in your body?	
4. Academic Check	• Have you seen a decline in your academic performance? • Are you frequently procrastinating or finding it hard to concentrate?	
5. Coping Mechanisms	• What coping techniques have you tried in the past when stressed? • Are there healthier coping mechanisms you'd like to explore?	
6. Time Management	• How do you currently manage your time, and do you find it effective? • Are there areas where you can improve your time management skills?	
7. Social Connections	• How strong is your support system, and who can you turn to during stressful times? • Do you actively engage with positive social connections?	
8. Stress Relief Toolkit	• Which stress management tools resonate with you? (Mindfulness, Physical Activity, Creative Outlets, etc.) • Are there any new techniques you're willing to try?	

After completing this checklist, take note of areas where you feel you might need to focus more on stress management. Remember, recognizing and addressing stress is a proactive step toward maintaining a healthy balance in your life.

MAKE A HUGE DIFFERENCE ... VERY QUICKLY!

Lessons about life lie in wait for you every single day if you're willing to embrace growth. That's a beautiful thing, and I know you're going to find the magic in it. This is your chance to help someone else discover the same joy.

Simply by sharing your honest opinion of this book and a little about your own experience, you'll help other teenagers find everything they need to build a strong foundation and move forward with confidence.

MAKE A LASTING IMPRESSION!

Thank you so much for your support. You're making a huge difference.

CONCLUSION

 "Life is not about waiting for the storm to pass but learning to dance in the rain."

— VIVIAN GREENE

As we draw the curtains on this journey through the maze of teenage challenges, it's time to reflect on the lessons learned, the obstacles overcome, and the tools acquired. In the realm of adolescence, where every day seems like a new adventure, our exploration aims to equip you with a compass—guiding you through the tumultuous waters of academics, extracurriculars, burnout, and stress. Let's take a moment to summarize the key insights and head on the final leg of this journey.

UNDERSTANDING THE TEENAGE JOURNEY

Our journey began with an exploration of time management—a skill that serves as the compass guiding your journey through teenagehood. Unveiling the mysteries of effective time management allowed you to wield the power to organize your schedule, optimize your time, and, ultimately, enhance your overall productivity.

Diving deeper, we looked into the enigma of procrastination. Exploring its intricacies, we identified its roots, understood its impact, and armed you with strategies to either avoid its clutches or confront it head-on. By demystifying procrastination, you gain the knowledge and tools necessary to minimize its influence on your productivity.

Our voyage through the teenage landscape also led us to the phenomenon of burnout. Recognizing the stages of burnout and understanding its potential triggers allowed you to navigate these treacherous waters with resilience. Armed with this awareness, you can now recognize the warning signs and take proactive measures to prevent or recover from burnout, ensuring a smoother voyage through the stormy seas of adolescence.

TIME MANAGEMENT: YOUR TRUSTY COMPASS

As we reflect on the journey, remember that time management is not merely a skill; it's your trusty compass, your guiding star. Whether you're facing the daunting challenge of balancing academic commitments or navigating the delicate world of extracurricular activities, effective time management remains your steadfast ally.

With the knowledge acquired, you now possess the ability to prioritize, plan, and optimize your time, ensuring a more balanced and fulfilling teenage experience.

THE PROCRASTINATION CONUNDRUM

Procrastination, the elusive adversary, loses its grip when met with understanding and strategy. Armed with insights into its psychology and practical techniques to overcome it, you now possess the tools to confront procrastination, turning it from a hindrance into an opportunity for growth.

As you traverse the maze of tasks and deadlines, remember that procrastination is not a permanent roadblock but a challenge you can conquer with resilience and determination.

NAVIGATING THE BURNOUT STORM

Burnout, a tempestuous force on the horizon, loses its potency when met with vigilance and self-care. Understanding the stages of burnout and recognizing its potential triggers empower you to navigate these stormy seas gracefully. By implementing preventive strategies and fostering a healthy relationship with your commitments, you can steer clear of burnout's tumultuous waves and maintain joy in your pursuits.

A SUCCESS STORY: YOUR TRIUMPH AWAITS

Every journey deserves a tale of triumph, a testament to resilience and growth. Consider the success story of Emily, a teenager who once grappled with the pressures of academia, the demands of extracurriculars, and the looming specter of burnout. Through diligent application of time management principles, she transformed her schedule into a well-organized roadmap. Emily confronted procrastination head-on, turning each deadline into an opportunity for accomplishment. Recognizing the signs of burnout early on, she adjusted her sails, seeking balance and recovery.

Emily's story is a beacon of hope, showcasing that with dedication, self-awareness, and the right tools, triumph over the challenges of teenage life is not just possible; it's inevitable.

KEY TAKEAWAYS: YOUR GUIDE TO TEENAGE SUCCESS

As we reach the conclusion of this odyssey, let's distill the wisdom gained into key takeaways:

- **Time Management Mastery**: Harness the power of effective time management to organize your schedule and optimize your time, enhancing overall productivity.
- **Procrastination Overcome**: Confront procrastination as an opportunity for growth, armed with knowledge and strategies to navigate the complexities of tasks and deadlines.
- **Burnout Resilience**: Navigate the stormy seas of burnout with resilience, recognizing its signs early on and implementing preventive strategies for a more balanced teenage experience.
- **Triumph Over Challenges**: Embrace the success stories of those who have triumphed over academic pressures, extracurricular demands, and burnout, knowing that your journey can be one of growth, resilience, and accomplishment.

A CALL TO ACTION: YOUR TEENAGE JOURNEY CONTINUES

As you stand at the conclusion of this teenage adventure, the journey doesn't end here—it's a continuation. Armed with the insights and tools acquired, your path forward is one of growth, learning, and triumph. Here's your call to action:

- **Implement and Reflect**: Apply the time management techniques, strategies to overcome procrastination, and burnout prevention methods in your daily life. Reflect on their impact and adjust your course as needed.
- **Seek Support**: Don't navigate this journey alone. Reach out to friends, family, mentors, and support systems. Share your challenges and triumphs, fostering connections that strengthen your resilience.
- **Review and Learn**: Take a moment to review what you've learned in this odyssey. Consider writing a brief review or reflection on the key takeaways. Share your insights with others to spread the knowledge.

YOUR REVIEW MATTERS

Finally, your thoughts and experiences matter. If this journey has resonated with you, consider leaving a review. Share your journey, your triumphs, and the lessons you've learned. Your review can be a guiding light for others heading on their teenage odyssey.

In closing, as you navigate the ever-changing landscape of adolescence, remember that you are not alone. This journey is a shared experience, and your ability to overcome challenges, embrace growth, and triumph is a testament to the incredible journey of teenage life.

REFERENCES

1. Renzulli, K. A. (2019, March 18). Completing this task first thing in the morning takes seconds—and it can make you more productive all day. [Web article]. CNBC. [URL: https://www.cnbc.com/2019/03/18/making-your-bed-first-thing-can-make-you-more-productive-all-day.html]

2. Vanbuskirk, S. (n.d.). The Mental Health Benefits of Making Your Bed. [Web article]. Verywell Mind. [URL: https://www.verywellmind.com/mental-health-benefits-of-making-your-bed-5093540]

3. Gulino, E. (n.d.). Research Says Making Your Bed in The Morning Sparks Productivity. [Web article]. House Beautiful. [URL: https://www.housebeautiful.com/lifestyle/fun-at-home/a26950790/research-making-bed-productive/]

4. Judd, B. (2023, June 13). Everyone in the world has 24 hours, but how do they spend their time? This is what the average human day looks like. ABC News Science. https://www.abc.net.au/news/science/2023-06-13/day-in-the-life-of-average-human-in-21st-century/102456844

5. Wolmark, M. (n.d.). Average Human Attention Span (Statistics). Golden Steps ABA. https://www.goldenstepsaba.com/resources/average-attention-span

6. Wilding, M. (n.d.). Work is Infinite, But Time is Finite. Medium. https://medium.com/publishous/work-is-infinite-but-time-is-finite-2caf219febe0

7. Sutter, P. M. (2019, January 9). Why Can't We Reverse the Arrow of Time? Discover Magazine. https://www. discovermagazine.com/the-sciences/why-cant-we-reverse-the-arrow-of-time

8. Siegel, E. (2020, April 4). Ask Ethan: Why Can't Time Be Reversed For Three-Body Systems? Forbes. https://www. forbes.com/sites/startswithabang/2020/04/04/ask-ethan-why-cant-time-be-reversed-for-three-body-systems/?sh= 13830f312a13

9. Gillihan, S. (n.d.). Why You Feel Like You're Always Running Out of Time — and How Not To. Everyday Health. https:// www.everydayhealth.com/columns/my-health-story/why-you-feel-like-youre-always-running-out-of-time/

10. Clear, James. ""Make Your Bed"." James Clear. Last modified August 3, 2021. https://jamesclear.com/great-speeches/make-your-bed-by-admiral-william-h-mcraven.

www.ingramcontent.com/pod-product-compliance
Lightning Source LLC
Chambersburg PA
CBHW070656130626
46553CB00005B/1730